Foreword

One can easily see how Dan Brown's novel, *The DaVinci Code*, has captured the imagination of millions of readers worldwide. It's all there...mystery, intrigue, conspiracy and action, not to mention the larger-than-life historical figures. But that's not all that's there. It also contains historical errors and misinformation that leads unsuspecting readers down a false path that undermines the very essence of the Christian faith. Dr. James A. Beverley has done a tremendous service for sincere truth seekers who desire to separate fact from fiction. As a defender of Biblical Christianity for over thirty years, Dr. Beverly has dedicated his life to providing solid, well researched answers to those in search of the real Jesus. I encourage you to carefully consider the true life, death and resurrection of Jesus that Dr. Beverly espouses in this book, because in the Truth of Jesus it's all there...the mystery of salvation, the intrigue of eternal life, the conspiracy of Satan, and the action Jesus took on our behalf. Truth can be stranger (but more exciting and life-changing) than fiction!

REV. RON MAINSE
President of Crossroads Christian Communications Inc.
Host of 100 Huntley Street

D1043014

Counterfeit Code

ANSWERING *THE DA VINCI CODE* HERESIES

Counterfeit Code

Answering The Da Vinci Code Heresies

James A. Beverley

BayRidge
B O O K S

Counterfeit Code: Answering The Da Vinci Code Heresies
Copyright ©2005 James A Beverley
All rights reserved
Printed in Canada
International Standard Book Number: 1-897213-01-8

Published by:
BayRidge Books
Willard & Associates Consulting Group
1-1295 Wharf Street, Pickering, Ontario, L1W 1A2
Tel: (416) 573-3249   Fax (416) 226-6746
E-mail: info@castlequaybooks.com
www.castlequaybooks.com

Copy editing by Larry Matthews
Cover Design by John Cowie, *eyetoeye, design*
Printed at Essence Publishing, Belleville, Ontario

Library and Archives Canada Cataloguing in Publication

Beverley, James A.

    Counterfeit code : answering the Da Vinci code heresies / James A.
Beverley.

Includes bibliographical references.

ISBN 1-897213-01-8

    1. Brown, Dan, 1964- . Da Vinci code. 2. Brown, Dan, 1964-
—Criticism and interpretation. 3. Jesus Christ—In literature.
4. Christianity in literature.
I. Title.

PS3552.R68139D33 2005   813'.54   C2005-901549-7

BayRidge
B O O K S

Table of Contents

Preface

My interest in *The Da Vinci Code*, the best-seller by Dan Brown, was raised first by all of the attention given to it on the Internet. I avoided reading the novel when it first came out because I was working on several major book projects throughout 2003. In early 2004 I finally read the novel and spent a lot of time studying its various theories. I also read *Angels & Demons*, Dan Brown's earlier and less controversial novel. I wrote most of the manuscript for this book in mid-2004 and then revised it several times through the rest of the year.

I owe a lot to those who have encouraged me over the last year about this project. My twin brother Bob has been very supportive. I have also been encouraged by my friends Kevin and Jill Rische, John Wilkinson, Rodney Howard-Browne, Beverly Matthews, Don Wiebe, John Kessler, Rick and Charis Tobias, Marta Durski, Ralston and Cheryl Nickerson, Massimo Introvigne, and Gordon Melton, my colleague at the Institute for the Study of American Religion.

As ever, I am grateful to my wife Gloria for her support and love. My adult children Derek and Andrea have also encouraged me, as has Julien, my son-in-law. It is always exciting to share my writing plans with my family. I also appreciate their patience with me, since getting to publication often takes longer than I predict.

I am grateful to Larry Willard for helping to put the book through publication. Larry Matthews has provided incredible editorial input. Thanks to Gus Henne, Renée VanderWindt, and Rikki-Anne McNaught for their work at Essence Publishing. I also appreciate the encouragement of Tyndale Seminary administration: Brian Stiller (President), Earl Davey (Provost), and Brian Cunnington (Academic Dean).

I invite readers to join in my analysis of the controversial theories of *The Da Vinci Code*. And, I would love to hear from any reader who engages with my book in a thoughtful and considerate manner. You can write me at my e-mail address below.

JAMES A. BEVERLEY
March 2005
jamesbeverley@sympatico.ca

Introduction

Author on a Mission

Dan Brown probably does not consider himself a missionary. That term conjures up images of faraway jungles and Protestant and Catholic ambassadors of the Christian gospel. Dan Brown is no Jesuit, and he does not sound like a missionary for the Southern Baptist Convention. However, the author of *The Da Vinci Code* is on a mission, whether he admits it or not. My concern is that he is unaware of the danger of his mission, not just for him but for everyone who believes the counterfeit code of his novel.

Sometime in the last few years Dan Brown heard of a radical ideology about Jesus Christ, Mary Magdalene, the Bible, and early church history. This new worldview involved allegations about secret societies and power plays by the Vatican. Some of the most famous figures in the worlds of art and science were also mentioned as crucial players.

Dan Brown appears to have embraced these new theories and has become a missionary for them. He did not spread the good news by preaching. He wrote a book. And that book has become the most widely sold adult novel in the entire history of humanity. *The Da Vinci Code* is now "the Bible" of this new gospel. And, Dan Brown has become its most famous apostle.

Readers of this book need to understand three important realities about *The Da Vinci Code* and its author. First, this is not just a novel. It is a novel that claims to be based on facts. The famous opening pages state that "All descriptions of artwork, architecture, documents, and secret rituals in this novel are accurate." If only Dan Brown would withdraw this misleading statement from his novel, there would be no need to worry about its false teachings about Jesus, Christian faith, Mary Magdalene, paganism, sexual rituals, the Bible, history, secret societies, Opus Dei, witchcraft, and Leonardo da Vinci.

Second, the novel is full of sloppy thinking and is based on seriously flawed research. *The Da Vinci Code* does deserve praise as a thriller novel, in my opinion, though a few reviewers have disliked it. But regardless of the literary merits, I sincerely believe Dan Brown owes his readers (especially his Christian ones) an apology for his inadequate research and careless thought, and for presenting as "fact" views that have been long discredited by experts.

Third, Dan Brown does not seem to be concerned enough to deal with evidence and arguments against his radical and harmful views. This is a moral, intellectual, and spiritual tragedy. As I will demonstrate in this book, Dan Brown has misled millions by following theories that have no credibility. His few public statements show little ability or desire on his part to address the strong case against his views.

Brown has basically said that he is glad that people are taking his book seriously. Fine, he still needs to take more seriously, and respond to, the abundant proof of experts that he has been duped by a few crackpot conspiracy theorists. In his defense, he is right that historically females have often been put down by the Church, but this is no justification for advancing a whole range of flawed views that are utterly foolish and untrue.

When I first heard about *The Da Vinci Code* I could not understand all the fuss about a novel. Now, after seeing the grave impact it is having on the Christian faith of many people, I know better. I have examined virtually every factual claim made in the novel. While we cannot look at every issue, this book lays out the evidence for the fact that Dan Brown is an unreliable guide for anyone interested in the truth about Jesus Christ and many of the related issues raised in *The Da Vinci Code*.

None of my criticisms are meant to deny Dan Brown's right to write or say what he believes, whether in a novel or otherwise. I defend his right to freedom of speech and freedom of religion. I admire his writing ability and his daily discipline as an author. Further, I believe that Christians should defend his liberty and do nothing that challenges his rights as a human being or as an American citizen.

Dan Brown appears to be a really nice guy. I do not question his sincerity or the motives of his writings. Given this, I hope he will show himself open enough to examine the evidence against his views and respond appropriately. Where he is wrong, he should admit it. Where he has damaged the faith of millions of Christians, he should apologize. He should not allow his unbelievable success as an author to blind him to his obligations to deal with the errors and false views that have made *The Da Vinci Code* a very dangerous model for looking at history and for studying religious issues.

Like Dan Brown, I am glad that his novel has led to serious engagement with very important spiritual and intellectual matters. However, it is very alarming that millions of people have used the strident claims of *The Da Vinci Code* as a rationale for their beliefs and views that have virtually no merit. Brown's views gain acceptance not only because people do not have the ability to investigate them, but mostly because they fit so conveniently with popular views of our day.

C. S. Lewis wrote that good philosophy must exist because bad philosophy needs to be answered. The same argument applies in relation to bad history and theology. I have written this book because I believe that *The Da Vinci Code* is built on bad research and flawed logic. I urge readers to now follow my arguments and examine the evidence for themselves.

Chapter One

Inventing a New Jesus

T he subject of more than 70,000 biographies, Jesus retains a
significance unmatched in human history.[1] However,
despite this ocean of ink, every generation debates that
ancient question—who is Jesus? Both *The Da Vinci Code* and Mel
Gibson´s controversial film *The Passion* have created a new round of
debate about the carpenter from Nazareth. *Who is Jesus?*—that
single query leads anyone, Christian or otherwise, to a host of other
questions about the Gospels, history, miracles, and revelation.

The Jesus of *The Da Vinci Code*

Dan Brown's rather eclectic picture of Jesus in his novel arises
out of the forces that have shaped him personally. He is obviously
affected by the Christian heritage in America, but he has also been
influenced by both skeptical philosophies and popular anti-traditional views of Jesus.

In keeping with his professed Christian faith, Dan Brown
treats Jesus with great respect in both *Angels & Demons* and *The Da
Vinci Code*. Teabing, one of the main characters in *The Da Vinci
Code*, states: "Jesus Christ was a historical figure of staggering
influence, perhaps the most enigmatic and inspirational leader

the world has ever seen." In *The Da Vinci Code* the word *Jesus* is used ninety-six times, all but once in a positive manner.

Sadly, the reverent treatment of Jesus is beside the point when contrasted with Brown's overall view of Christ and the church. The key assertions that undergird the novel destroy classical Christian convictions about Jesus Christ. The novel's portrait of Jesus and the Christian faith can be captured in twenty statements:

1. *The traditional Gospels are not reliable*
2. *Christianity, like all religions, is based on fabrication*
3. *The miracles of Jesus are not to be taken literally*
4. *Almost everything the Church Fathers taught about Jesus is inaccurate*
5. *The Church suppressed the true gospel provided in Gnostic scriptures and in the Dead Sea Scrolls*
6. *Jesus is not divine*
7. *The real Jesus was a nature-loving pagan*
8. *The earliest Jews and Christians engaged in sexual rituals and were right to do so*
9. *Jesus was married to Mary Magdalene*
10. *Jesus and Mary had a child named Sarah*
11. *The remains of Mary Magdalene represent the Holy Grail*
12. *Constantine invented the divinity of Jesus*
13. *Constantine created the traditional Bible*
14. *The dynasty of Jesus and Mary merged with French kings*
15. *These truths were suppressed by power-hungry leaders through Church history*
16. *These truths about Jesus were preserved by a secret society known as the Priory of Sion*
17. *These truths were also taught through hidden symbols in the art of Leonardo da Vinci*
18. *The real Jesus would identify with witchcraft and paganism*

19. Many views of Jesus were copied from pagan religion

20. Nothing in Christianity is original

Anyone, Christian or not, should be able to recognize that the above paradigm represents an all-out assault on what the vast majority of Christians—past and present—believe about Jesus and the gospel. In May 2004 Dan Brown told a writers' group in New Hampshire that he almost included in *The Da Vinci Code* the view that Jesus was not actually crucified.[2]

Dan Brown and his defenders often misunderstand why critics are upset about issues surrounding Mary Magdalene. This is not simply about whether or not she was married to Jesus. *The Da Vinci Code* goes far beyond the suggestion of marriage. In the novel Mary Magdalene becomes the central character in a larger paradigm that both explicitly and implicitly undermines the Biblical picture of Jesus Christ.

Brown's theories should create both intellectual and spiritual alarm. First, Christians have every right to vigorously object to the direct, wholesale denial of major Christian teachings about Jesus. Brown is not saying that the Church has misunderstood a few items, major or not. No, Christians have been mistaken on virtually all major beliefs, and *The Da Vinci Code* is supposed to set it all straight.[3] No wonder Christians are upset.

Further, anyone who values academic honesty and intellectual rigour should note the hazards involved in accepting the theories of *The Da Vinci Code*. Brown's fondness for conspiracy theories, his support for unfounded historical judgments, and his gullible embrace of the wildest theories present a pattern that must be resisted by anyone, Christian or not, who values careful research and thought.[4]

Dan Brown is not wrong because his views are controversial or anti-traditional. Rather, Brown's errors arise out of his careless thinking and naive embrace of outlandish theories. I don't expect readers to simply take my word on this critique of Brown. The evidence is what matters. So, let's examine Brown's theories that

Christianity represents "nothing" original and that early Christians copied from pagan religions.

Nothing Original in Christianity?

The claim that there is "nothing" original in the Christian tradition is obviously extreme. It is impossible to accept at face value given the incredible impact that Jesus made on history. If there was nothing original in Christianity, why did the early Christian movement make such an impact?

Consider the positive affirmation about Jesus noted earlier. "Jesus Christ was a historical figure of staggering influence, perhaps the most enigmatic and inspirational leader the world has ever seen." Anyone who fits that description must be original in some way in order to deserve such praise. Further, any new development in a religious tradition always represents something original. The degree to which Christianity represents a departure from classical Judaism makes it unique.

A Copycat Jesus?

Christianity's relationship with paganism is a fascinating and complex topic. This covers not only interpretive issues in the New Testament but also the ways in which the early Church Fathers reacted to ancient paganism. In the New Testament Paul addressed whether Christians were allowed to eat meat that had been offered to idols in pagan worship. Later Christian leaders had to figure out the proper response to Greek philosophy and to what extent Christians could duplicate some elements of pagan worship.

For now, let's think about the argument that Jesus was really a pagan. This would be one of the last things that would occur to a reader of the New Testament. What anyone can see in reading the Gospels is that Jesus is firmly rooted in his Jewish heritage. He is presented clearly as a child of the synagogue, as a rabbi of the Jewish scriptures, as a son of Jewish parents, and as a participant in the wider Jewish community.

One of the major conclusions reached by almost all New Testament scholars, whether conservative or liberal, whether Protestant, Catholic, Jewish, or secular, is that Jesus will never be understood until he is recognized as a product of his Jewish environment.[5] In other words, any tendency to see him as a pagan must be met with a stubborn recognition that Jesus was a Jewish teacher—a monotheist to the core.

The Da Vinci Code tries to argue that early ideas about Christ were copied from pagan mythology. The idea of Christ's Virgin Birth is said to be borrowed from the story of the miraculous conception of Horus by his mother Isis. The novel also states that "the pre-Christian God Mithras—called *the Son of God* and *the Light of the World*—was born on December 25, died, was buried in a rock tomb, and then resurrected in three days."

The novel makes two major errors—one of logic and one of fact—in presenting its case. First, there is an error in logic. Assume that Dan Brown is accurate in reporting that pagans believed before the time of Jesus that the Greek god Horus was conceived supernaturally by his mother Isis. This only proves similarity of the basic idea and not copying from one tradition to the next. There is no evidence that Matthew and Luke had ever heard of Horus or Mithras.[6]

On this, one must also clearly maintain the radical difference between legend and historical reality. There is really no comparison between a legendary story of a mythical pagan god and a real event involving an actual person like Jesus. No scholars of the ancient world believe that Horus or Mithras are historical figures. Virtually everyone knows that Jesus actually existed.

Of course, Christians need to be careful to not overstate the differences between pagan myths and Gospel facts. Some widespread legends can find their ideal fulfillment in the Gospels. This is what C. S. Lewis, the famous English professor, discovered in his conversion to Jesus. He found that his love and appreciation of ancient mythology found its true home in the historical reality of the life of Christ.[7]

The second error by Dan Brown on the copycat theory is factual—a mistaken representation of the pagan legends. *The Da Vinci Code* paints a superficial picture so that the parallels with Christian teaching seem more striking than is actually the case. In the novel, Teabing omits mentioning that in one Egyptian legend Horus cut off the head of his mother. Another legend states that Isis was both wife and sister to Osiris, Horus's father.

Misrepresentation is even more obvious in the statements about Mithras. First, Mithras was not born on December 25th or any other particular date, since he is not a real figure of history. Second, scholars of Mithraism do not claim that there is even a legend of a birth on December 25th.[8] Third, Mithraic legends do not have him rising from the dead. Finally, the overall mythology about Mithras arises from a radically different view of the world than the one provided in the life and teachings of Jesus.

Conclusion

As we will examine later, it is entirely reasonable that Christians and others look for Jesus in the only secure source about him—the Gospels and the other writings of the New Testament. In any historical study, pride of place goes to the earliest and primary documents. Apart from a few references in Roman and Jewish histories, the New Testament constitutes the sole source by those who either knew Jesus directly or wrote within decades of his death. If the Gospels are not reliable, there is no hope of knowing the truth about Jesus.[9]

Who is Jesus? Read the Gospels once or a thousand times, in any version, and it is obvious what is clear on its pages. He is human, descended from David, born of a virgin, a worker of miracles, a prophet, the Son of God, the promised Messiah, and the incarnation of God. He was a powerful preacher, exorcist, prayer warrior, and healer. He was demanding, gracious, powerful, gentle, courageous, and loving. He liked parties, hung around with sinners, adored children, and loved the outsider. He died for our sins and rose bodily from the dead. This is the gospel that changed the world.

The Da Vinci Code presents a different gospel, one that depends on belief in hidden Gospels that were suppressed by the Vatican and the emperor Constantine. Dan Brown believes that these suppressed Gospels provide amazing truths about Mary Magdalene and the sacred feminine. These spiritual realities have been preserved through the centuries by a secret society and embodied in the artwork of Leonardo da Vinci. Is this really the case? Let's examine the evidence.

Chapter Two

Mary Magdalene: A New Goddess?

*T*he *Da Vinci Code* has much to say about Mary Magdalene. More prominent in the novel than Jesus, she is pictured as a tragic and misunderstood figure, emerging as the heroine of early Christianity and authentic spirituality. Before we examine the portrait of Mary in the novel, it will help to know what the New Testament has to say about her.

Mary Magdalene in the New Testament

The name Mary is used of seven different women in the New Testament.[10] (1) Mary, the mother of Jesus, (2) Mary Magdalene, (3) Mary of Bethany, sister of Martha and Lazarus (Luke 10:38–42), (4) Mary, the mother of James and Joses (Matt. 27:55–61), (5) Mary, the mother of John Mark (Acts 12:12), (6) Mary, wife of Clopas (John 19:25), and (7) Mary of Rome (Rom. 16:6).

According to the New Testament, we know the following about Mary Magdalene:

- She was from Magdala, a town on the southwest of the Sea of Galilee
- Jesus cast seven demons out of her (Luke 8:1–2)
- She became a follower of Jesus (Luke 8:1–3)

- She was part of a group of women who supported Jesus financially (Luke 8:2–3)
- She witnessed the events surrounding the death of Jesus (Mark 15:40, John 19: 25)
- She was one of the first witnesses to the resurrection of Jesus (John 20:11–18)

Mary Magdalene in *The Da Vinci Code*

Dan Brown shows no hesitation in building a whole new complex of theories about Mary Magdalene. His viewpoint will be examined under ten different claims:

Claim #1

Mary Magdalene was not a prostitute. "That unfortunate misconception is the legacy of a smear campaign launched by the early Church. The Church needed to defame Mary Magdalene in order to cover up her dangerous secret—her role as the Holy Grail."

Response

Brown is correct in saying that Mary was not a prostitute. However, there was no smear campaign against her by early Church leaders. The view that she was a prostitute arose simply because some early Catholic leaders thought that Mary Magdalene was the prostitute mentioned in one account in the life of Jesus.[11]

Claim #2

The early Church omitted references to Mary Magdalene as the Bible was edited. Church leaders were troubled by the "earthly elements" in the life of Jesus and were especially upset about Mary Magdalene.

Response

As is often the case, *The Da Vinci Code* makes bold claims without evidence. To know that Mary Magdalene was edited out of the Bible one would have to possess early copies of the four Gospels that contain the alleged unedited story of her life. Dan Brown cannot produce any documentation for his theory. First-year students of logic will recognize this as a clear example of a logical fallacy—arguing from silence to make an unprovable claim.

Claim #3

Mary Magdalene was married to Jesus. The novel claims that there are "countless references" to their union in ancient history and that the topic "has been explored *ad nauseam* by modern historians."

Response

There is no evidence in any documents of the first century that Jesus was married. Further, there are not "countless references" to the marriage of Mary and Jesus in ancient history. Contrary to Dan Brown's claim, there is no unambiguous text about the marriage of Jesus even in the Gnostic Gospels. Finally, modern historians have hardly ever explored this topic, although *The Da Vinci Code* will now make it mandatory for historians to do so.

There would be nothing intrinsically wrong with the idea that Jesus was married to Mary Magdalene. Christian faith does not rise or fall on Jesus' marital status. However, building a religious ideology without regard for careful historical research is spiritually futile and intellectually dishonest. Since there is no valid historical evidence that Jesus was married, the novel's portrait of Jesus and Mary Magdalene as husband and wife has no foundation in reality.

Claim #4

The disciples were jealous of the relationship between Jesus and Mary. This was especially true of St. Peter. The novel states that Peter was discontented "over playing second fiddle to a woman."

Response

The attack on St. Peter is part of the overall anti-Catholic bias of *The Da Vinci Code*.[12] Again, there is no evidence from the time of Jesus that the disciples were jealous of Mary Magdalene. This is a case of pure invention, found first in the Gnostic literature that dates more than a century after the death of Jesus.

Claim #5

Mary Magdalene was from the tribe of Benjamin and from a royal lineage.

Response

There is nothing in early Jewish or Christian writings from the first century that give any suggestion about the tribal roots of Mary. Likewise, the idea that she has a royal lineage is a purely modern idea, stemming largely from Michael Baigent, Richard Leigh, and Henry Lincoln, the authors of *Holy Blood, Holy Grail*. They picked up the idea from Pierre Plantard, the eccentric French conspiracy theorist and creator of the Priory of Sion theories that Brown has accepted uncritically.

Claim #6

Mary Magdalene has been identified through history via pseudonyms: *the chalice* and *the Holy Grail*. She has also been known as *the Rose*—a term that has "ties to the five-pointed pentacle of Venus" and also serves as "an anagram of Eros, the Greek god of sexual love." According to the novel, "the Rose has always been the premiere symbol of female sexuality" and when it blossoms it "resembles the female genitalia."

Response

The novel contradicts itself. First it is argued that the dominant historical tradition has painted Mary as a prostitute. Then the novel suggests that she has been known through history as a sex goddess. Which is it—reformed prostitute or sex goddess? Linking Mary Magdalene, a first-century Jewish woman, with pagan ideologies about sex is grossly inaccurate.

Claim #7

Mary Magdalene was seated next to Jesus at the Last Supper. This assertion is supposedly based on Leonardo's famous painting *The Last Supper*. *The Da Vinci Code* presents the discovery in this fashion: "Sophie examined the figure to Jesus' immediate right, focusing in. As she studied the person's face and body, a wave of astonishment rose within her. The individual had flowing red hair, delicate folded hands, and that hint of a bosom. It was, without a doubt…female."

Response:

Since a whole chapter is devoted to Leonardo da Vinci later in this book, only a brief comment is necessary here. There is an enormous difference between interpreting the famous painter's artwork and deciding what is historically true about Mary Magdalene. Even *if* Leonardo painted Mary next to Jesus in his famous work, this tells us nothing about whether Mary sat next to Jesus in real life.

Claim #8

Mary was pregnant at the time of the death of Jesus. Joseph of Arimathea, her uncle, helped her move to France. There she gave birth to a girl that she named Sarah. Mary and Sarah found refuge in the Jewish community in France. "Countless scholars of that era chronicled Mary Magdalene's days in France."

Response

There is absolutely no valid historical documentation for any aspect of this claim. There is no mention in the Christian Gospels or the Gnostic material that Mary got pregnant, moved to France, had a child named Sarah, or was protected by any Jewish community. It is totally untrue that "countless scholars" write about these ideas. I don't think Dan Brown could name even one recognized scholar who tries to prove these wild theories.

Claim #9

"The quest for the Holy Grail is literally the quest to kneel before the bones of Mary Magdalene. A journey to pray at the feet of the outcast one, the lost sacred feminine."

Response

As we will examine later, *The Da Vinci Code* presents a brand new theory about the Holy Grail. Only in the last few years has anyone ever proposed that the quest for the Grail is about kneeling at the feet of Mary Magdalene. The Grail legends are just that—legends! Dan Brown has only clouded the issue with his own legends and myths about the Holy Grail.

Claim #10

The bones of Mary and the secret documents about her have been protected since the 11th century by the secret society known as the Priory of Sion.

Response

Almost every historical claim unique to *The Da Vinci Code* rests on Dan Brown's belief in the reality of the Priory of Sion. His case for this will be examined in detail in a separate chapter. For now, let me just say that readers have every reason to be very skeptical of his theory.

Background to a Legendary Kiss

Dan Brown gets the idea of kissing between Mary and Jesus from the Gospel of Philip, one of the famous Gnostic documents. Here is the relevant quote: "the companion of the Savior is Mary Magdalene. But Christ loved her more than all the disciples, and used to kiss her often on her mouth. The rest of the disciples were offended... They said to him, 'Why do you love her more than all of us?'" (Gospel of Philip, 63.32–64.5).

Readers of Brown's novel are not told anything about the Gospel of Philip or about the larger context of the statement. On the latter, Brown simply avoids mentioning the many eccentric and bizarre theories of this Gnostic Gospel. Nor does he mention ideas from the Gospel of Philip that are incompatible with Brown's purposes. For example, the Gospel of Philip states: "Compare the soul. It is a precious thing and it came to be in a contemptible body." This anti-body teaching is entirely out of sync with Brown's emphasis on sexuality.

Brown also never faces the question of the historical reliability of the Gospel of Philip. Some scholars believe that the document dates from the third century, that is, almost 200 years after the death of Christ. The earliest suggested date for this Gnostic Gospel is after A.D. 160.

Modern Religion and Mary Magdalene

Given the success of *The Da Vinci Code*, it should come as no surprise that the figure of Mary Magdalene has become increasingly popular. There is a revival in interest in the Gnostic scriptures about her. Entire books are now devoted to her, and she is the object of increasing worship and devotion. Many Web sites are built around her as the central figure.[13]

The pagan Church of the Way worships both Jesus and Mary Magdalene. This is embodied in the language of their creed, which reads in part:

> *I believe in Mary Magdala, an Incarnation of the Divine Feminine who did anoint the Son of Man to seal His Divine Kingship; to prepare Him for His death, descent into Hell and Resurrection.*
>
> *For Yeshua and His Bride the Magdala did come in the flesh, were wed, and together showed us The Way to freedom from suffering, to balance, to wholeness and union with Our Creators.*
>
> *I acknowledge their continued presence among us. They are co-Redeemers in joint priest- and priestess-hood leading all back into kinship with the Creative Godhead.*

Lesa Whyte, a contemporary pagan author, wrote in *Sage Woman*: "Mary Magdalene is the closest thing I can conceive of as a Goddess. She is my vision of divine wisdom, feminine glory and sensuality. My dedication is much more a result of personal revelation and meditation than anything set down by a scribe hundreds of years ago. I have dedicated myself to her service in the manner appropriate to any pagan woman who would dedicate herself to a deity."

She continues: "She has helped me gain an understanding of death, and of perfect love. The new millennium, for me, will truly bring a new comprehension of what it means to be a woman, a mother, a sister, a daughter, a lover, and a follower of The Magdalene."

Conclusion

Thanks to Dan Brown there is a renewed interest in Mary Magdalene. In fact, a case could be made that he has almost single-handedly changed perceptions about her. Christians should be grateful to Dan Brown for correcting the mistaken notion that Mary Magdalene was a prostitute. However, this benefit is virtually eradicated by the historical blunders that he makes about her.

His assertions about Mary Magdalene are provided without evidence. Apart from his point about her not being a prostitute, there are no historical reasons to support his wild theories about Mary. The only explanations for the popularity of his views about her is that people have been fooled by his confident rhetoric and that they do not care to examine the historical record about her.

Chapter Three

The Bible and the Ghost of Constantine

*T*he *Da Vinci Code*, the best-selling novel of all time, raises serious questions about the Bible, the best-selling book of all time. Although the novel uses the word *Bible* only twenty-six times, Brown stages a wide-ranging assault on its integrity. When the dust settles, readers who grant Brown any credibility are left with grave doubts on the inspiration of the Bible, its composition, and the uniqueness of its message.

This negative impact is achieved in part because Brown's characters speak with utter confidence. Uninformed readers would never imagine that some of the accusations against Scripture are only worthy of a reply because of the popularity of the novel.

The Inspiration of Scripture

The first significant comment about the Bible begins with the tantalizing claim: "And everything you need to know about the Bible can be summed up by the great canon doctor Martyn Percy." This is spoken by the fictional character Teabing, the novel's expert on the Holy Grail, but the novel is referring to a real person. I actually know Martyn Percy, who has taught at Cambridge and is now at Oxford.

The character Teabing quotes Percy this way: "The Bible did not arrive by fax from heaven." Teabing then makes his own observations:

> The Bible is a product of *man*, my dear. Not of God. The Bible did not fall magically from the clouds. Man created it as a historical record of tumultuous times, and it has evolved through countless translations, additions, and revisions. History has never had a definitive version of the book."

Three criticisms need to be made about this negation of divine inspiration of the Scriptures. First, though the novel quotes Percy correctly, he told me that he disagrees with the way his words are interpreted in *The Da Vinci Code*. Here is what Canon Percy wrote to me:

> The Bible is "not a fax from heaven" is a quote correctly attributed to me in a number of newspapers all over the world. The quote is used to stereotype and critique fundamentalists and their literalist view of revelation, in which scripture passes from God to text, without due acknowledgement being made for the role of culture, translation or indeed any other agency.
>
> Dan Brown appears to think that the compilation of the canon was either more of an accident or a conspiracy. I don't, obviously, agree with this. I think that the books we have in the Bible present themselves as true, because they testify uniquely to who Jesus was and is, and the life of the Holy Spirit in the church today.

Many evangelical Christians would have a stricter view of inspiration than Canon Percy. Yet his affirmation of the basic integrity of the Bible places him at a great distance from the outlook of *The Da Vinci Code*. The debate here is not about whether or not there are minor errors in the Bible. No, the claims of Dan Brown's novel undermine the basic integrity of the Bible itself.

Second, the fictional character Teabing also uses faulty logic in his discussion of the Bible. As Percy implies above, that the Bible did not arrive by fax or drop from the clouds proves nothing about whether God is the ultimate inspiration behind human authorship.

Finally, the novel creates a completely misleading impression through overstatement. Although the Bible has been translated into many languages and scholars debate the details of additions and revisions, the debate does not really affect the basic integrity of the Old and New Testaments. When we read the Bible today in any language we are reading virtually the same text used by Martin Luther, Thomas Aquinas, St. Augustine, and the earliest Church Fathers.[14]

The Ghost of Constantine

In a few pages *The Da Vinci Code* makes the most astounding claims about the emperor Constantine, relating both to his personal faith, his manipulation of Christian tradition and pagan religion, and his role in manufacturing a new Bible and destroying the truth about Jesus Christ.

After Teabing refers to "eighty Gospels" about Jesus, Sophie asks: "Who chose which Gospels to include?" Teabing replies: "Aha! The fundamental irony of Christianity! The Bible, as we know it today, was collated by the pagan Roman emperor Constantine the Great." Teabing scoffs at the notion that Constantine was a Christian. "Hardly. He was a lifelong pagan who was baptized on his deathbed, too weak to protest. In Constantine's day, Rome's official religion was sun worship… and Constantine was its head priest."

According to the novel, Constantine simply made a pragmatic political decision to unify the Roman Empire under Christianity. "Constantine was a very good businessman. He could see that Christianity was on the rise, and he simply backed the winning horse." *The Da Vinci Code* continues by noting Constantine's brilliance in converting Roman citizens to Christianity. "By fusing pagan symbols, dates, and rituals into the growing Christian tradition, he created a kind of hybrid religion that was acceptable to both parties."

The novel then deals with Constantine's role at the famous Council of Nicea in A.D. 325. Teabing tells Sophie: "My dear, until *that* moment in history, Jesus was viewed by his followers as a mortal prophet, a great and powerful man, but a man nonetheless. A mortal." Sophie asks: "Not the Son of God?" Teabing replies: "Right."[15]

He goes on to say that Jesus' divinity was the result of a relatively close vote, in a move designed to consolidate Vatican power.

> By officially endorsing Jesus as the Son of God, Constantine turned Jesus into a deity who existed beyond the scope of the human world, an entity whose power was unchallengeable. This not only precluded further pagan challenges to Christianity, but now the followers of Christ were able to redeem themselves only via the established sacred channel—the Roman Catholic Church.

The Da Vinci Code makes another bold declaration:

> Because Constantine upgraded Jesus' status almost four centuries after Jesus' death, thousands of documents already existed chronicling His life as a mortal man. To rewrite history books, Constantine knew he would need a bold stroke. From this sprang the most profound moment in Christian history... Constantine commissioned and financed a new Bible, which omitted those gospels that spoke of Christ's human traits and embellished those gospels that made him godlike. The earlier gospels were outlawed, gathered up, and burned.

Any individual who resisted Constantine's Bible was labeled a heretic, according to Dan Brown. *The Da Vinci Code* even claims that "the word *heretic* derives from that moment in history" and that "almost everything our fathers taught us about Christ is *false*." It is no wonder that *The Da Vinci Code* has created a theological storm.

The Truth about Constantine

Despite the bravado in Teabing's pronouncements, the picture he presents of Constantine and the Council of Nicea is a concoction of half-truths and outright errors, mixed with enough small nuggets of truth to sound convincing. First, consider the claim that Constantine was hardly a Christian but rather a lifelong pagan who was too weak to protest his baptism near his death.

Even readers unfamiliar with Constantine's life might ask: "Who would dare to force the Roman emperor to be baptized against his will?" In actual fact, Constantine willingly chose baptism. Dan Brown will find it very difficult to name any historians of the Roman Empire who will validate his claim of a forced baptism.[16]

The Da Vinci Code neglects to inform its readers that Constantine is said to have undergone a dramatic conversion to Christ while engaged in military battle. While scholars dispute the details of the conversion, they do not dispute Constantine's change of mind about Christianity.

The reality of conversion provides the best explanation for Constantine's advocacy for Christians and his private and public statements in favor of a Christian worldview. Why would Constantine care about the detailed deliberations of the Council of Nicea if he was not a Christian?

Errors in *The Da Vinci Code*

Contrary to what Dan Brown states:

- Jesus was viewed as divine long before Constantine
- The word *heretic* existed long before Constantine
- The Council of Nicea did not invent the divinity of Jesus
- The Council did not make the Roman Catholic Church the only channel of redemption
- Constantine did not finance a new Bible
- Constantine did not burn other Bibles

Jesus as divine—Pre-Constantine testimony to belief in the divinity of Jesus is easy to find. All anyone has to do is read material by and about Christians from the second and third centuries. For example, Athenagoras, a Christian philosopher, wrote to Emperor Marcus Aurelius in the late second century and declared to him: "The Christians worship the Father, Son, and Holy Ghost."

In his *Exhortation to the Heathen* Clement of Alexandria, writing in the second century, referred to Jesus as "the Savior, the Divine Word, He that is truly most manifest Deity, He that is made equal to the Lord of the universe; because He was His Son, and the Word was in God."

The origin of *heresy* and *heretic*—It is easy, likewise, to discover that the word *heretic* was used long before Constantine. Irenaeus wrote *Against Heresies*, a major critique of false teachings, in the second century. He was the bishop of Lyons in France. Tertullian, another Church Father, wrote a whole book called *The Prescription Against Heretics* in the late second century or early part of the third. Here is one of his statements: "But let us rather be mindful of the sayings of the Lord, and of the letters of the apostles; for they have both told us beforehand that there shall be heresies."[17]

Jesus' divinity not an "invention"—The bishops at the Council of Nicea did not invent the deity of Jesus. Rather, they met in order to decide how best to formulate the long-standing tradition in the Church that Jesus is the Son of God. Constantine did not force the bishops to create a divine Jesus. Rather, he wanted the bishops to come to agreement about the nature of His divinity.

It is also important to remember that the bishops at the Council all agreed on the humanity of Jesus. Any attempt to deny his humanity would have been met with fierce resistance. In the end, the false and simplistic picture presented in *The Da Vinci Code* is an insult to the memory of Constantine and the work of the bishops at the Council.

Canon Percy wrote this to me about these issues:

> The idea that Jesus was "upgraded" by Constantine from human to Son of God is not a view that makes sense of the weight of evidence we have from the gospels, or from the history and theology of the first four centuries of the church.

Roman Catholicism not set as the "only way"—The novel is also wrong in its suggestion that the Council made the Roman Catholic

Church the "only established sacred channel" for salvation. This idea fails on several grounds. First, it is a simplistic reading of Church history, making it sound like everything changed at the Council in terms of what Christians thought about the Catholic Church. Second, this interpretation is anachronistic since it is using later Catholic notions of exclusivity from the high Middle Ages and reading them back into the fourth century.

No Bible by Constantine—No Bible was financed by Constantine. By the final decade of the fourth century most Christians in both the East and West recognized all of the books we know now as the New Testament. In fact, most books of the New Testament were accepted among Christians by the middle of the second century. Finally, by the time of Constantine, the so-called Gnostic Gospels had little appeal to most Christian leaders.

The evidence for these points is presented in great detail in the first volume of *The Cambridge History of the Bible*.[18] Constantine is not mentioned as even a minor player in the formation of the New Testament. There is likewise no proof that the emperor ordered the burning of any Bibles, though he may have ordered the destruction of the writings of Arius, the theologian who denied the eternal pre-existence of Jesus at the Council.

While *The Da Vinci Code* has prodded many people to study anew how Christians came to accept the books that make up the New Testament, it is unfortunate that Dan Brown's novel makes so many untrue and careless statements about the topic. Granted, the Bible did not drop like a fax from heaven. However, the Bible also did not come from Constantine, but from Jews and Christians who were witnesses of God's work in Israel and in Jesus.

Chapter Four

Hidden Gospels?

O ne of the most important issues raised by *The Da Vinci Code* is what should constitute the authentic Gospels about Jesus Christ. As Dan Brown knows, most Christians believe that the question is easily solved. "Doesn't everyone know that Matthew, Mark, Luke, and John are *the* Gospels?"

This rhetorical question means little to Brown, since he has with complete confidence offered the world a totally different theory. As we noted earlier, *The Da Vinci Code* argues that the traditional Gospels are highly inaccurate. Instead, the true picture of Jesus Christ comes allegedly from the Dead Sea Scrolls and the Gnostic Gospels.

Gnosticism and the Gnostic Gospels

Through his novel Dan Brown has brought more attention to Gnosticism than anyone in the entire history of humanity. Scholars in Gnostic studies are being queried about their specialty simply because of *The Da Vinci Code*. Sales have increased dramatically for books about the Gnostic Gospels.

"The Gnostic Gospels" is a shorthand way of referring to documents from early church history that reflect a Gnostic understanding of both Judaism and Christianity. The most famous collection of Gnostic documents is often referred to as "the Nag Hammadi Library." These texts were discovered in Egypt in 1945. The Library is named after the town in Egypt near where the discovery was made.

The most important and famous document from the Library is *The Gospel of Thomas*. This Gospel and the other documents were published in 1977 by James M. Robinson under the title *The Nag Hammadi Library*.[19] Robinson is one of the most famous scholars of Gnosticism. He is the former director of the Institute for Antiquity and Christianity and Professor Emeritus at the Claremont Graduate School in California.

In addition to James Robinson, modern awareness of Gnosticism owes much to the Princeton scholar Elaine Pagels. She is known widely for her book *The Gnostic Gospels*, published in 1979, and her recent book *Beyond Belief: The Secret Gospel of Thomas*.[20] Pagels is sympathetic to a Gnostic understanding of Christianity.

Up until the discovery of the documents in Egypt, our knowledge of Gnosticism came either from secondhand sources, mainly the writings of the early Church Fathers, or from a few Gnostic documents discovered in prior archaeological investigation. The most famous Gnostic text outside of the Nag Hammadi collection is *The Gospel of Mary*. Unfortunately, large sections are missing from that document.

The Main Features of Gnosticism

The term *Gnosticism* comes from the Greek word *gnosis*, which means knowledge. Probably the most important aspect of the Gnostic Gospels is the emphasis on knowledge as direct experience. Gnosticism claims that the gathering of knowledge, the most important activity of humans, is about inner light and self-discovery. This is why some people see the New Age movement as a revival of Gnosticism.

It is also commonly understood that the Gnostic literature

teaches that it is the elite who gain enlightenment. This explains why the Gnostic Gospels are often referred to as "the secret Gospels." This fits well with the teaching that true enlightenment comes only to those few with special abilities or insight.

The Apocalypse of Adam, one Gnostic text, provides an example of a claim to special inside knowledge. "This is the hidden knowledge of Adam, which he gave to Seth, which is the holy baptism of those who know the eternal knowledge through those born of the word and the imperishable illuminators, who came from the holy seed: Yesseus, Mazareus, Yessedekeus, the Living Water."[21]

Gnosticism also places emphasis on the self. This is seen most radically in the symmetry between the individual and God. It is not that Gnostics do not believe in God; rather, they merge personal awareness with the divine. Pagels puts it this way in *The Gnostic Gospels*: "Self-knowledge is knowledge of God; the self and the divine are identical."

Responding to Dan Brown and Gnosticism

1. What must be recognized at the outset is the need to distinguish the teaching of the Gnostic Gospels from the ideology of Dan Brown. It is very regrettable that Elaine Pagels has not provided a sustained critique of Brown's views of Gnosticism.[22] He has radically distorted modern understanding of the "Christian" Gnostic tradition through careless interpretation, selective quotation, and misplaced emphases.

Even *if* the Gnostic Gospels were adopted as authentic, this would *not* lead to the *The Da Vinci Code's* version of Christianity. In the novel Mary Magdalene comes across as more significant than Jesus, contrary to the texts of Christian Gnosticism. It is very significant that Dan Brown pays far more attention to her than to Jesus.

Further, the novel places much more emphasis on sex than one finds in any Christian Gnostic text. Unlike *The Da Vinci Code*, references to sexual issues are usually made with subtlety and a sense of propriety. It is quite impossible to imagine

Valentinius or any other Gnostic Christian leader engaging in the sex ritual that takes centre stage (literally!) in the religion defended in the novel.

2. The novel is also very misleading through its simplistic treatment of the Gnostic Gospels. The novel gives any uninformed reader the impression that the Gnostic documents offer a comprehensive and thorough introduction to the life and teaching of Jesus. The Gnostic literature is actually boring and confusing and provides little historical information about Jesus. This becomes obvious when one actually reads *The Gospel of Mary* or *The Gospel of Philip* or any other Gnostic Gospel.

The Apocalypse of Adam, for example, provides no significant information about Jesus. Instead, it offers rambling and confusing pronouncements about Adam and Eve, Noah and his sons, and God's judgments. Typical of the document is this passage:

> And the seventh kingdom says of him that he is a drop. It came from heaven to earth. Dragons brought him down to caves. He became a child. A spirit came upon him and brought him on high to the place where the drop had come forth. He received glory and power there. And thus he came to the water.

3. *The Da Vinci Code* seriously distorts the historical issues related to Gnosticism. The novel adopts a very simplistic view of the tensions between orthodox Christians and the Gnostics. The Gnostics are presented as the great champions of truth and goodness while orthodox Christians are dismissed as power-hungry chauvinists. There are no nuances and no possible counter-argument.

Even a quick reading of serious reviews of major books about Christian Gnosticism reveals how completely Dan Brown distorts the true historical complexities. Sympathetic reviewers of Elaine Pagels's new book *Beyond Belief* know that the issues under discussion often involve very debatable claims.

Consider the analysis from Birger Pearson in *The New York Review of Books*. Here is what is said about *The Gospel of Thomas*, the

main text behind Pagels's book: "We have no clear idea who com-
posed it or compiled it, and scholars differ widely over its literary
status (a collection of sayings, excerpts from a lost commentary, a
'gospel'), its religious character ('gnostic,' 'mystical,' Jewish, anti-
Jewish, philosophical)."

This is also true, the review continues, of "its date (mid-first
century to late second century), original language (Greek or
Syriac), its place of origin (Syria, Palestine, Egypt), and its relationship to the gospels of the New Testament canon (dependent
on them or independent)."[23]

Dan Brown has repeatedly stated in interviews that his novel
is based on serious research. If he is a serious researcher, he
should be haunted by the verdict of James Robinson about his
views. In an interview for Dan Burstein's *Secrets of the Code*,
Robinson states: "It is clear to me that Dan Brown doesn't know
much about the scholarly side of things in my field and he sort of
fudges the evidence to make it more sensational than it is."[24]

4. Readers of the *The Da Vinci Code* need to know the price paid
if one adopts the Gnostic Gospels as the only guide about Jesus.
These Gospels show very little interest in the actual life of Christ.
The only way in which the Gnostic Gospels have any power is if
one assumes the basic integrity of the traditional Gospels.

One of the real tragedies of *The Da Vinci Code* is that readers
who are spiritual seekers may take Dan Brown's false interpretation and defense of the Gnostic Gospels at face value. It will be
assumed that these documents provide a great picture of Jesus.
However, the Jesus of the Gnostic Gospels is a rather dull and
confusing figure, prone to endless rambling. *The Book of Thomas
the Contender* contains many examples such as this:

> The savior said, "All bodies [...] the beasts are begotten [...] it is
> evident like [...] this, too, those that are above [...] things that are
> visible, but they are visible in their own root, and it is their fruit
> that nourishes them. But these visible bodies survive by
> devouring creatures similar to them with the result that the bodies
> change. Now that which changes will decay and perish, and has

no hope of life from then on, since that body is bestial. So just as the body of the beasts perishes, so also will these formations perish. Do they not derive from intercourse like that of the beasts?

5. Dan Brown's understanding of Gnosticism is also wrong-headed because of his careless historical analysis. It is universally recognized among scholars that the vast majority of Gnostic texts were written long after the traditional Gospels. Why would anyone think that the Gnostic documents, dating from the second and third century, have better historical value than the traditional Gospels that date within decades of the death of Jesus?

It is rather ironic that Dan Brown argues for the historical credibility of the Gnostic Gospels when it is obvious that the Gnostic authors have no interest in eyewitness testimony, primary source documents, and other aspects of careful historical writing. The last thing Gnostic writers cared about was providing accurate historical testimony to the incredible figure of Jesus. For that, one has to turn to the Gospels of the New Testament.

The Da Vinci Code and the Dead Sea Scrolls

The novel states boldly that the famous scrolls prove that trust in the Bible is misguided. Both the Gnostic scriptures and the Dead Sea documents are called "the earliest Christian records." It is then stated that it is troubling that "they do not match up with the Gospels in the Bible."

The Scrolls represent one of the most well-known discoveries in recent archaeology. Most of the documents found at the Dead Sea were discovered in 1947 and some in the next few years. The vast majority of the Scrolls were in fragment form, though an entire copy of the book of Isaiah was also unearthed. Altogether, the fragments are from about 800 different documents.

The Scrolls have aroused controversy because of outrageous conspiracy theories that have emerged about the documents. Also, a few eccentric scholars have used the documents to argue against the truth of Christianity. Scholars have also had significant debate about both the importance and meaning of these ancient texts.

Part of the battle over the Scrolls arose simply because the scholars originally working on translation and publication took so long to do so and were very stingy in allowing access to the original documents. Thankfully, this all changed in 1991 when the Huntington Library announced an open access policy.

Most scholars date the documents from 250 B.C. to A.D. 100. For forty years there was one dominant theory about the Scrolls. It was believed that the Scrolls were the work of the Essenes, an ascetic religious community near Qumran in the area of the Dead Sea. In the last fifteen years scholars have grown more skeptical about this theory. Now, it is commonly argued that the Scrolls are from many different traditions in Judaism and, to a far lesser extent, the early Christian movement.

Contrary to *The Da Vinci Code*, the Dead Sea Scrolls do not call into question the truthfulness of Christianity. The novel is completely misguided in making such a claim. Most of the Scrolls pre-date the time of Christ, and the entire set of fragments has little to do with Christianity.[25]

Conclusion

There are no valid reasons to accept Dan Brown's speculations about hidden Gospels. He has a wrong understanding of Gnostic material and misunderstands the Dead Sea Scrolls. His rejection of the reliability of the four traditional Gospels leaves him with no historical basis for his reckless views of Jesus, Mary Magdalene, and the earliest Christians.

Chapter Five

Secret Societies and the Holy Grail

Everybody loves secrets, and Dan Brown loves telling them. The now famous opening page of *The Da Vinci Code* declares under the title *Fact*:

The secret society of the Priory of Sion was founded in 1099, after the First Crusade. In 1975, parchments referred to as "Dossiers Secrets" were discovered at the Bibliothèque Nationale, which mention the names of certain members of the Priory, including Sir Isaac Newton, Botticelli, Victor Hugo and Leonardo da Vinci.[26]

The Da Vinci Code also claims that the Order of the Knights Templar was actually a creation of the Priory of Sion. Under the guise of protecting Jerusalem during the Crusades, the Templars' actual job, according to the novel, was looking for ancient documents buried beneath the Temple. The Templars found this treasure in four huge chests. One of the major discoveries was the actual diary of Mary Magdalene, again according to the novel. After the Knights Templar Order was crushed in 1307, the documents were retained by the Priory of Sion.

As a further development about the Priory, it is also argued that a modern French priest named Father Berenger Saunière discovered secret treasure and ancient parchments near his church in the village of Rennes-le-Château. The village is now a celebrated destination of Priory enthusiasts and has become widely known in occult circles. There are dozens of books about the "mysteries" of Rennes-le-Château and the "strange" wealth of Father Saunière.

Critics of Saunière contend that he was removed from his role as parish priest simply because he engaged in "trafficking in masses." Before Vatican II, Roman Catholic priests were allowed to accept money for performing masses. However, Church officials discovered that Saunière engaged in a form of fraud through false advertising about masses for both the living and the dead. Father Saunière died in 1917, but he remains the subject of endless speculation.[27]

How should we approach Dan Brown's conspiracy theories? First, his ideas about secret societies deserve study, even if only because he has made the idea of secret societies a firm conviction among millions of his readers who know no different. The stunning success of *The Da Vinci Code* demands investigation into the murky world of secret societies.

Second, not all secret societies are created equal. For example, everyone knows that there really are Masonic lodges and there really is a Roman Catholic group known as Opus Dei. However, there is no consensus about the Illuminati's actual existence in contemporary society. Obviously, conspiracy theories involving secret societies must be examined on a case-by-case basis..

Third, readers of *The Da Vinci Code* should be wary about Dan Brown's self-confidence about his own findings on secret societies. If these groups are as powerful and mysterious as Brown suggests, it is surely hard to imagine that he could unearth the truth about every group he studies while writing fiction. Further, if Dan Brown is right about the Illuminati and Opus Dei, he should be under a witness protection program.

The Priory of Sion

Dan Brown's theories about an ancient Priory of Sion are basically worthless. He has been fooled by superficial arguments and shallow evidence about the alleged super-spiritual secret society. Readers should note how easy it is to be fooled by the appearance of study and research. *The Da Vinci Code* actually lists the twenty-six Grand Masters of the Priory of Sion from 1188–1963. This sounds impressive until one tries to find any hard historical evidence that any of the alleged Masters, like Isaac Newton, were actually involved in this secret society.[28]

Given the confident manner in which *The Da Vinci Code* speaks of the Priory, it is quite shocking to see the extent of the failure in Brown's research. Where did he go wrong?

Brown did not examine the credibility of Pierre Plantard, the original source behind contemporary legends about the Priory of Sion. Plantard is the eccentric French conspiracy theorist who invented most of the mythology about the Priory. His decades of lies were exposed in 1993 by a French court when Plantard was forced to admit to his scam about the Priory of Sion.

Dan Brown is also careless in his rhetoric about alleged ancient documents about the Priory. As noted earlier, the novel states: "In 1975, parchments referred to as 'Dossiers Secrets' were discovered at the Bibliothèque Nationale." There is a different wording about this on Brown's Web site: "In 1975, Paris's Bibliothèque Nationale discovered parchments known as Les Dossiers Secrets." Whatever wording is chosen, the facts tell a different story:

- The famous French Library did *not* discover any parchments about the Priory in 1975 or any other year.
- "Les Dossiers Secrets" are *not* parchments discovered in 1975. Rather, it is the title given to various documents made up in the 1960s.
- There are *no* ancient parchments in existence about the Priory of Sion.

On these points, I challenge Dan Brown to provide any ancient documents that support his views. Sadly, Brown simply accepted popular modern legends about the Priory of Sion. Dan Brown marred his own credibility by drawing only from authors obsessed with myths and conspiracies. When Brown first encountered the tales of the Priory of Sion, he owed it to himself and his readers to explore the exhaustive research archive of Paul Smith on Plantard and the Priory.[29]

He also owed it to his readers to do a study of scholarly views of the book *Holy Blood, Holy Grail*, which provides the basic argument behind Dan Brown's conspiracy theories. *The Times Literary Supplement* called the book "worthless" and "silly." Serious scholars never use the book as a guide to history, whether about French dynasties or Christian issues.

Does all this mean there is no Priory of Sion? Plantard did form an association under that title in 1956. However, it was not created as a secret society and dealt with local political and social issues. It was only in 1961 that Plantard claimed that the Priory of Sion was an ancient society. This second version of the Priory gained popularity after the publication of Gérard de Sède's *L'Or De Rennes* in 1967. Plantard invented another version of the Priory story in 1984 and then renounced everything in 1993.

Q&A

1. Why not trust Plantard about the Priory of Sion?
- Throughout his life Plantard engaged in fraud and deception
- Plantard offered three different and contradictory explanations of the Priory of Sion
- Plantard fabricated the claim that he was descended from the royal bloodline of Mary and early French kings
- Plantard tried to make the case that he was the true king of France
- Plantard admitted in court that he had made up the whole mythology about the Priory of Sion

2. How did Plantard end up in court?
When Plantard reinvented the Priory legend in 1989 he made a new list of Grand Masters. He made the costly mistake of including the name Roger-Patrice Pelat in the list. Pelat was, at the time of his death, involved in a major financial scandal.

Thierry Jean-Pierre, the judge who investigated the scandal, allowed Plantard to testify in court. He also had Plantard's home searched. In the end, Plantard admitted that he had lied about the Priory of Sion as an ancient order and lied that he was the true king of France. Plantard disappeared from the public light for the rest of his life.

3. Do Pierre Plantard and Father Beranger Saunière appear in The Da Vinci Code?

No, not directly. Their last names are used. The murdered curator at the Louvre is given the last name of Saunière. Sophie, the heroine of the novel, is said to have descended from the Plantard and Saint-Clair families. Dan Brown has adroitly connected his narrative directly to two major real-life figures central to the rise of the legends about the Priory of Sion.

4. Why should Paul Smith be trusted in his critique of Plantard?

Smith's Web site contains in-depth and extensive documentation. He provides readers with primary documents, a comprehensive chronology, an extensive bibliography, and translations of rare French material. Smith also follows evidence carefully and does not engage in the complicated flights of reason so common in literature about the Priory of Sion.

5. How do Priory advocates deal with Paul Smith?

Often Smith is simply ignored. His character is sometimes called into question. At one time Plantard used forged documents to try to discredit Smith. At other times there is a grudging admission that his case is compelling, but then the argument is made that there are still mysteries connected with Plantard and Saunière that point to ancient truths about the Priory of Sion.

The Priory and the Holy Grail

As *The Da Vinci Code* acknowledges, the Grail is normally understood as the cup from the Last Supper of Jesus Christ. According to legend, the Grail was used at the crucifixion to catch the blood of Jesus. One legend even states that the Grail was brought to Britain by Joseph of Arimathea. The legendary knights of King Arthur made their main goal in life to find the sacred cup.

The first written text about the Grail comes from about A.D. 1180 in a French verse romance by Chrétien de Troyes called the "Conte del Graal" ("Story of the Grail") or "Perceval." A.D. Perceval is the name of the French knight who must find the Grail. Various versions of the Grail legend circulated in France and other parts of Europe for the next three centuries. Sir Thomas Malory's "Morte d'Arthur" is one of the more famous works and dates from the late 15th century. According to Malory, Sir Galahad is the principal knight in the majestic quest.

The legends do not regain their hold on popular conscience until the 19th century. Then, various artists (George Frederic Watts), writers (Alfred Lord Tennyson and Scott), and composers (Richard Wagner) bring to life the power and mystery of the earlier Grail legends. Here are some of Tennyson's famous lines:

> *"O just and faithful knight of God!*
> *Ride on! the prize is near."*
> *So pass I hostel, hall, and grange;*
> *By bridge and ford, by park and pale,*
> *All-arm'd I ride, whate'er betide,*
> *Until I find the holy Grail.*

Generally, most historians do not think there was a King Arthur as described in the famous legends. At best, some scholars think there may have been an early English military figure that became the starting point for the development of the legends. It must be remembered that even the traditional legends contradict themselves.[30]

The Priory and the Knights Templar

The Knights Templar is a religious military order founded in the early 12th century. Hugues de Payens, a French Knight, led eight comrades in the campaign to protect pilgrims to the Holy Land. Baldwin II, the king of Jerusalem, provided shelter for them in the royal palace. In 1139 Pope Innocent II placed the Knights under direct Vatican authority.

The order grew in size and financial power through the 13th century. King Philip IV of France was reportedly jealous of the Templars and may have believed rumours about heretical aspects in Templar initiation rites. In any case, on October 13, 1307, every Templar in France was arrested. Pope Clement V banned the order five years later. Templar property was given to the various states or to the Hospitalers, another military movement. Jacques de Molay, the Grand Master of the Templars, was burned at the stake in 1314 after he had recanted his confession of heresy that had been obtained through torture.

After the death of de Molay, the work of the Knights Templar was carried on by the Knights of Rhodes and the Knights of Malta. Historians have continued to debate whether Templar initiations were ever heretical. Generally, recent scholarship has been sympathetic towards the Knights Templar, believing that de Molay and his comrades were victimized by both French and Vatican power.

While certain mysteries remain about the demise of the Order, the plot of *The Da Vinci Code* depends on the bogus theory that the Knights Templar were actually engaged in protecting the bones of Mary Magdalene. To believe this, one has to accept further baseless theories about Father Saunière, the Priory of Sion, the Merovingian dynasty, and the Holy Grail. Accepting these additional views demands placing trust in a discredited conspiracy theorist whose fables were exposed by the courts of France.

Conclusion

The Da Vinci Code is built on an elaborate hoax about the Priory of Sion. I do not believe Dan Brown knew better when he wrote the novel. I cannot imagine he knew about the research archive of Paul Smith. Rather, he trusted the wild fancies of *Holy Blood, Holy Grail* and thought he had discovered solid gold. Sadly, he has shown no interest in dealing with the enormous evidence against his novel's so-called facts on these topics.

Likewise, his theories about the Holy Grail are built on total speculation that the Grail is the bones of Mary Magdalene. In all of the writing on the Grail through history, this has never been suggested. This is a modern invention, as is the theory that the Knights Templar really worked at protecting Mary Magdelene's remains, physical and literary. This is another idea that is without any historical support.

Chronology Related to the Priory of Sion	
1852	Birth of Father Berenger Saunière
1885	Saunière became parish priest in Rennes-le-Château
1909	Saunière suspended as priest for "Trafficking in Masses"
1917	Saunière died.
1917	Properties left to Marie Denarnaud (1868–1953)
1920	Birth of Pierre Plantard
1937	Plantard formed anti-Jewish and anti-Masonic movement known as the French Union
1942	Plantard started *Vaincre*—a journal sympathetic to Hitler
1953	Sentenced to prison for six months on fraud charges
1956	Founded the Priory of Sion—a social organization
1956	Noel Corbu (1912–1968) spread Saunière treasure legend
1957	Priory dissolved as legal entity
1960	Plantard promoted himself as a psychic
1961	Plantard re-created Priory as ancient secret society
1962	Gérard de Sède presented Plantard as expert on Templars
1964	Plantard claimed that he is a descendant of Merovingian kings
1967	*Dossiers Secrets d'Henri Lobineau* compiled by Philippe Toscan du Plantier

1967	Gérard de Sède authored *L'Or De Rennes* (from a manuscript by Plantard)
1972	Plantard married Anne-Marie Cavaille
1973	Plantard interviewed by Jean-Luc Chaumeil
1975	Plantard began referring to himself as "Plantard de Saint-Clair"
1979	Plantard appeared in BBC2 documentary on "The Shadow of Templars"
1982	*Holy Blood, Holy Grail* published
1983	Plantard began attack on Jean-Luc Chaumeil
1984	Plantard announced resignation from Priory of Sion
1989	Third version of Priory introduced by Plantard
1993	Plantard admitted in French court to lies about Priory of Sion
1996	BBC2 documentary discredited Plantard
2000	Plantard died on February 3
2003	Dan Brown released *The Da Vinci Code*

Chapter Six

The Real Leonardo da Vinci

In December 2002 I stood with my son Derek in the Louvre in Paris before the *Mona Lisa*. While gazing at this, the most famous painting in the world, I would never have imagined that its creator, Leonardo da Vinci, would soon be a major figure in a worldwide publishing phenomenon. I also would never have guessed that Dan Brown, a novelist, would be the one to provide the inside "truth" about Leonardo, his life, religion, and art—and about Christ and Christian faith itself.

Leonardo and the Priory of Sion

The major statements about Leonardo and the Priory are presented with no hint of uncertainty. The novel's hero Robert Langdon addresses its heroine Sophie.

> "I've written about this group," he said, his voice tremulous with excitement. "Researching the symbols of secret societies is a specialty of mine. They call themselves the Prieure de Sion— the Priory of Sion. They're based here in France and attract powerful members from all over Europe. In fact, they are one of the oldest surviving secret societies on earth.
>
> "Da Vinci presided over the Priory between 1510 and 1519

as the brotherhood's Grand Master. The Priory has a well-documented history of reverence for the sacred feminine."

"You're telling me this group is a pagan goddess worship cult?

"More like *the* pagan goddess worship cult."

Despite the total conviction in Langdon's eyes, Sophie's gut reaction was one of stark disbelief. *A secret pagan cult? Once headed by Leonardo da Vinci?* It all sounded utterly absurd.

The claim that Leonardo was Grand Master of a secret pagan cult is, in fact, "utterly absurd." We have already noted that there are no ancient parchments about the Priory of Sion. Also, there is absolutely no primary evidence from the time of Leonardo that gives any indication that he was involved in a pagan cult. This is a secret so well buried that no experts of Renaissance art claim to have any knowledge about it. On this issue, Dan Brown lives in fantasy.

In addition to reading public replies from Leonardo specialists about *The Da Vinci Code*, I consulted with art historians in both North America and Europe. Some of these experts did not want to be quoted publicly but were willing to give me their professional opinion privately. There was complete agreement that Leonardo had nothing to do with a pagan sex cult.

James Beck, a professor at Columbia University, gave me permission to quote him. He stated in an interview: "What Brown gets right is known by scholars. Anything that is unique to his book about Leonardo is nonsense." He said that it was "total nonsense" that Leonardo was the Grand Master of a pagan sex cult. He said he could hardly imagine that Dan Brown actually believed many of the claims advanced in *The Da Vinci Code*.[31]

General Claims about Leonardo da Vinci

The novel states that Leonardo has "always been an awkward subject for historians," particularly those in the Christian tradition. In reply, two things need to be noted. First, Christian historians do not write about Leonardo, simply because he has little to do with the basic narrative of church history. Contrary to Brown, Leonardo da Vinci is not a major player in the Christian tradition.[32]

Second, it must also be realized that any awkwardness by historians about Leonardo has nothing to do with the speculations about him in Dan Brown's novel. Art experts have their debates about specific paintings. However, these experts never give serious consideration to claims that Leonardo was really the super agent in an ultra-secret society designed to protect the bones of Mary Magdalene.

The claim that he was a "flamboyant homosexual" is rather overstated. The idea that Leonardo may have been gay is based on one rumour about him when he was a young man. There is no solid evidence from his contemporaries that he was sexually active, either with men or with women. When one reads about Leonardo, what emerges most clearly is that he was obsessed, not with sexual issues but with the world of art, mathematics, engineering, military planning, and science.

Contrary to what the novel states, Leonardo did not accept hundreds of lucrative Vatican commissions. There is some evidence he might have accepted one! It is true that he was a bit of a "prankster," and the novel correctly argues that he was the most skilled artist in using particular painting techniques.

Leonardo and Spiritual Issues

The novel provides a very contradictory portrait of Leonardo's spirituality. On the one hand, it is argued that Leonardo was "an exceptionally spiritual man." Then, contrary to this, he is said to have been selfish and to have lived "a lavish lifestyle." Which is it? The novel claims that Leonardo da Vinci was skeptical of the New Testament, but we know that he requested the last rites of the Roman Catholic Church near his death.

In the novel Teabing attempts to prove that the artist was skeptical about the New Testament through two quotations from Leonardo himself. "Many have made a trade of delusions and false miracles, deceiving the stupid multitude!" The second quotation is equally blunt. "Blinding ignorance does mislead us. O! Wretched mortals, open your eyes."

When these quotations are compared to what is written in the actual notebooks from Leonardo, they do not appear to be about the Bible. The first is said to be an accusation against the ancient practice of alchemy, and the second quotation is from a general observation about morality. Neither seems to have anything to do with the New Testament![33]

Apart from this point, something very obvious emerges when Leonardo's notebooks are analyzed. He seems to have no interest in goddess worship. It is important to realize that these notebooks provide us with insight into the private world of Leonardo. One of the notebooks contains about 250,000 words and covers hundreds of topics. The word *goddess* appears only once in the entire document!

Consider again the claim that he was a flamboyant homosexual. If this was the case, how can Dan Brown explain Leonardo's alleged frequent lucrative Vatican commissions? Did the ultra-powerful Vatican, ever searching for heretics to torture, not realize that Leonardo was engaged in homosexual acts? Of course, if the Vatican did not know that he was gay, and there is no written evidence, obviously it is advisable, hundreds of years later, to be silent or agnostic on the topic of his sexual identity.

Further, if Leonardo is a self-centred hedonist, how could he possibly occupy the central role in one of the most important spiritual societies allegedly ever known to humanity? Remember that the goal of the Priory of Sion is to protect the remains of Mary Magdalene (the true Holy Grail) and the precious documents about her. The truth about Jesus and the sacred feminine is in the hands of this ultra-secret organization. Would its members risk everything they stand for by making a self-centred hedonist their Grand Master?

Leonardo and His Paintings

The Last Supper

Dan Brown makes some very remarkable claims about Leonardo's famous painting *The Last Supper*. Contrary to the novel, the painting is not "an astonishing tribute to the sacred feminine." As all art scholars contend, the painting deals with the impending betrayal of Jesus. Leonardo wanted us to think about the complexities of human guilt as he pictures the disciples asking who will turn their back on Jesus. The painting is not about the sacred feminine. Rather, it is about the sinful male apostles.

Ludwig Heinrich Heydenreich captures the essence of the The Last Supper in his article on Leonardo in the Encyclopaedia Britannica. Heydenreich was Director of the Central Institute for the History of Art in Munich from 1947–1970 and an expert on Leonardo's work.

> Leonardo's Last Supper (1495–98) is among the most famous paintings in the world. In its monumental simplicity, the composition of the scene is masterful; the power of its effect comes from the striking contrast in the attitudes of the 12 disciples as counterposed to Christ. Leonardo portrayed a moment of high tension when, surrounded by the Apostles as they share Passover, Jesus says, "One of you will betray me."

Renaissance art specialists have never claimed that it is Mary Magdalene seated next to Jesus. It was standard convention for all painters to have John, the beloved disciple, sitting next to Jesus. And, most important, Renaissance artists, Leonardo included, always pictured John with long hair and a beautiful face. The reason we are fooled by the suggestion that it is Mary Magdalene is because we use current standards of masculinity to judge Renaissance standards.

The argument of Dan Brown that the letter M is hidden in the painting is simply a product of imagination. Critics of The Da Vinci Code have gone back to The Last Supper and shown how other letters can be pictured by simply looking for the right angles that make up this or that letter of the alphabet. Again, even if everyone knew there was a letter M in the painting, why not say that it stands for Mary the mother of Jesus?

The Mona Lisa

Dan Brown makes a poor case for reinterpretation of the *Mona Lisa*. The notion that the painting is a combination of both male and female features has received very little endorsement from experts in Renaissance art. Further, the idea that the term *Mona Lisa* is an anagram from the Egyptian god Amon and the famous goddess Isis is completely out of character with Leonardo's overall interests. No one in Leonardo's day made any mention of this possibility.

The Virgin of the Rocks

When I first read about the two different versions of Leonardo's portrait of the Christ child, I thought that *The Da Vinci Code* might be on solid ground. After all, some Renaissance artists were preoccupied with images from the pagan world, so it was easy to imagine that Leonardo might have offended his sponsor. I realized that the only way to settle this was to look at the two versions of the painting. The earliest painting, the more controversial one, is at the Louvre, while the other is in the National Museum in London.

To my astonishment, when I looked at both paintings what hit me was the close similarity between them and not the differences. There is simply no way to demonstrate that the Virgin Mary and Uriel threaten John in the first painting. Further, the real differences between the two paintings can be explained completely with reference to common Christian themes picked up by Leonardo as he did the second work. The first painting created conflict between Leonardo and his sponsor. There was no major scandal, and to this day Renaissance scholars do not know for sure what created the difficulties.

Conclusion

Leonardo da Vinci's works have been radically misunderstood by Dan Brown. The only way to accept the viewpoint of *The Da Vinci Code* is to ignore the artist's own testimony about his work and the observations of his contemporaries. Further, Brown's speculations can only be supported if one totally ignores the assessment of Renaissance art experts, who have universally dismissed his allegations about Leonardo.

One of the ways to respond to the extravagant claims of *The Da Vinci Code* is to read biographical essays or books about Leonardo. Those studies, based on attention to the thousands of pages from Leonardo's own hand, reveal a brilliant artist utterly consumed with advancing human knowledge about painting, anatomy, engineering, architecture, hydrology, military technology, physiology, mathematics, and flight. The last thing that comes to mind is that Leonardo was preoccupied with being Grand Master of a pagan sex cult.

Life of Leonardo da Vinci	
April 15, 1452	Birth near Vinci (now part of Italy)
c. 1467	Apprenticed to Andrea del Verrocchio
1472	Joined painters' guild in Florence
1482	Moved to Milan (sponsor: Duke Ludovico Sforza)
1482	Studied of higher mathematics
c.1483–1486	Worked on *The Virgin of the Rocks*
1493	Clay model of equestrian statue on public display
1495–1498	Worked on *The Last Supper*
1499	Left Milan
1500	Returned to Florence
1502	Worked as architect/engineer to Cesare Borgia
1503	Returned to Florence
1503f.	Studied anatomy and hydrology
c. 1503–1506	Worked on the *Mona Lisa*
1508	Settled in Milan
c. 1508	Created second *Virgin on the Rocks*
1513–1516	Worked in Rome
1516–1519	Served under King Francis I in Cloux, France
May 2, 1519	Death in France

Chapter Seven

Sex at the Altar

Whatever else *The Da Vinci Code* offers, Dan Brown provides the reader with an interesting and radical portrait of goddess worship, witchcraft, and sex ritual. One reason for the novel's popularity might be an underlying sexual theme, although there are times that things seem to be overdone. For example, there is the serious suggestion in the novel that some of the architectural designs in Gothic cathedrals were meant to tell us about the most private parts of the female body.[34]

Early in the novel we are given clear signals that Sophie, the heroine, had witnessed her grandfather taking part in some form of sex rite. Later Robert Langdon gently probes her memories of the event and provides explanation and defense of the traumatic episode. Here are some of the key moments in the narrative:

> She turned suddenly back to Langdon, her eyes welling with emotion. "I don't know what I saw."
>
> "Were both men and women present?" After a beat, she nodded. "Dressed in white and black?"
>
> She wiped her eyes and then nodded, seeming to open up a little. "The women were in white gossamer gowns...with

golden shoes. They held golden orbs. The men wore black tunics and black shoes."

Langdon strained to hide his emotion, and yet he could not believe what he was hearing. Sophie Neveu had unwittingly witnessed a two thousand-year-old sacred ceremony. "Masks?" he asked, keeping his voice calm. "Androgynous masks?"

"Yes. Everyone. Identical masks. White on the women. Black on the men."

"It's called Hieros Gamos," he said softly. "It dates back more than two thousand years. Egyptian priests and priestesses performed it regularly to celebrate the reproductive power of the female." "Hieros Gamos is Greek," he continued. "It means *sacred marriage*."

"The ritual I saw was no marriage."

"Marriage as in *union*, Sophie."

"You mean as in sex."

"No."

"No?" she said, her olive eyes testing him.

Langdon backpedaled. "Well…yes, in a manner of speaking, but not as we understand it today."

After this rather amazing introduction to sexual rituals, *The Da Vinci Code* continues with some astounding claims about such rituals in early Jewish and Christian practice:

Admittedly, the concept of sex as a pathway to God was mind-boggling at first. Langdon's Jewish students always looked flabbergasted when he first told them that the early Jewish tradition involved ritualistic sex. In the Temple, no less. Early Jews believed that the Holy of Holies in Solomon's Temple housed not only God but also His powerful female equal, Shekinah.

Men seeking spiritual wholeness came to the Temple to visit priestesses—or *hierodules*—with whom they made love and experienced the divine through physical union. The Jewish tetragrarnmaton YHWH—the sacred name of God—in fact derived from Jehovah, an androgynous physical union between the masculine Jah and the pre-Hebraic name for Eve, *Havah*.

"For the early Church," Langdon explained in a soft voice, "mankind's use of sex to commune directly with God posed a serious threat to the Catholic power base. It left the Church out of the loop, undermining their self-proclaimed status as the *sole* conduit to God. For obvious reasons, they worked hard to demonize sex and recast it as a disgusting and sinful act. Other religions did the same."

The novel states that "more than a dozen secret societies around the world—many of them quite influential—still practiced sex rites and kept the ancient traditions alive"—such as portrayed in the controversial movie *Eyes Wide Shut*. In that film Tom Cruise discovers a Manhattan group participating in such ritual. (*The Da Vinci Code* argues that the film mangled the details of the ceremony.)

These crucially important assertions play into a larger ideological claim about authentic Christianity, witchcraft, and goddess worship. *The Da Vinci Code* would have us believe that the true gospel of Jesus Christ was essentially the celebration of sex rites. Thus, the earliest Christianity was a continuation of alleged Jewish sexual rituals, ones that were similar to those of early paganism and the practices of witches, ancient and modern.

According to Brown, this version of Christianity was exemplified by Mary Magdalene and the Gnostic Gospels. This true Christian faith was crushed by sex-hating, chauvinistic leaders of the Church. Allegedly, Mary Magdalene's heirs in France preserved the true gospel, and this sacred sexual gospel was also protected by witches through the centuries.

The Da Vinci Code deals with some of the most complex issues in religion, history, and human sexuality and gender by making very radical pronouncements with an air of utter authority. Examining the ideas one by one in order will help assess the integrity of components that make up the ideology of the novel.

In the balance of this chapter, we will pursue separate lines of inquiry about ancient Judaism, goddess religion, and Hieros

Gamos. In the next chapter we will examine Dan Brown's claims about witchcraft and the occult.

Ancient Judaism and Sex Ritual

What *The Da Vinci Code* proclaims about sexual ritual in ancient Judaism is simply staggering. The idea that orthodox Jewish priests would have condoned sexual ritual in Solomon's temple is basically ludicrous. The documents of Hebrew scripture contain constant admonitions against the practice of the sex rites of neighbouring pagan religions. Further, early Jews did not believe that *Shekinah* was the female partner of God in the Holy of Holies or anywhere else. The N*elson's New Illustrated Bible Dictionary* notes that the word *Shekinah* is not even in the Hebrew or Christian scriptures.

Dan Brown gets his view from a distorted understanding of an aspect of *late* Jewish Kabbalism, the very esoteric and mystical element of Judaism. Kabbalistic Jews refer to a feminine aspect of God's manifestation in the world but never deny the unity of God. God has no partner, sexual or otherwise.

Likewise, the claim that YHWH is derived from *Jehovah* is totally false. It is actually the reverse. *Jehovah* is a popular, though faulty, English vocalization derived from the four-letter Hebrew word for God. Given that *Jehovah* is an English term, it is completely misleading to speak of "an androgynous physical union between the masculine Jah and the pre-Hebraic name for Eve, *Havah*."

I could find no reference to Jah in any Bible dictionary, encyclopedia about Judaism, or any other reference work. *Havah* is not a pre-Hebraic term but the English vocalization of the Hebrew word for Eve. Havah has nothing to do with any part of the English word *Jehovah*. Scholars normally pronounce YHWH as *Yahweh* and not *Jehovah*.[35]

The Ancient Goddess and Hieros Gamos

Dan Brown dons rose-coloured glasses to view ancient goddess worship. In the process, he engages in a very selective reading of history and neglects to address some very crucial questions, particularly in relation to Hieros Gamos. Goddess worship was a reality before and during the time of Christ. Likewise, we now live in a time of renewed interest in goddess religion in the West; many thousands of people worship Isis, Aphrodite, and other goddesses. These devotees may refer to themselves as pagans, witches, Druids, or New Agers.

The Da Vinci Code makes several major errors in its portrait of ancient goddess religion. First, it ignores important distinctions between forms and understandings of ancient paganism. This creates the impression that there is deep uniformity in ancient pagan rites. This is simply untrue.

Readers of The Da Vinci Code should ask tough questions about the numerous deities worshipped in ancient times.

Consider this list of goddesses: Aphrodite, Asherah, Artemis, Astarte, Brighid, Demeter, Diana, Freya, Gaia, Hera, Ishtar, Isis, Juno, Kali, Laverna, Lilith, Ma'at, Minerva, Ostare, Persephone, Venus, and Vesta. Are these deities real? All of them? If not, how does one decide which are real? Are we to believe the stories of the goddesses? Aphrodite is said to be the elder twin of the sun. Is this true? Laverna is the goddess of thieves. Does she really protect criminals?

Second, and more important, the novel never acknowledges the negative aspects of paganism, ones that should cause any reader, pagan or otherwise, to think seriously about the wisdom of choosing paganism, especially its ancient form, as the template for spirituality. Some feminist scholars are starting to realize that the picture of an earlier gentle matriarchal world dominated by goddess worship is an illusion.

In ancient times the worship of the goddess was no guarantee of liberation for women. In fact, a priestess in the pagan religions was often simply a temple prostitute. She would be better off to worship as a Jew in the synagogue or a Christian in the community of the church. This fact alone is a stinging correction to the novel's wild postulations about ancient pagans.

This raises a third failure related to *The Da Vinci Code* and ancient paganism. Brown provides a simplistic picture of Hieros Gamos, the sex rite described at the outset of this chapter. He also opens before us a very dangerous interpretation and defense of sexual ritual. It is almost impossible to imagine that he has thought through the implications of his novel's ideological posture about Hieros Gamos.

The novel would have readers believe that Robert Langdon knows the precise details of Hieros Gamos, evidenced by the fact that he immediately relates Sophie's description (women in white gossamer gowns and golden shoes and men in black tunics and black shoes) with the ancient sex rite.

However, even scholars sympathetic to pagan religion admit that descriptions about Hieros Gamos from the ancient world are very vague. Consider this verdict from Miriam Harline, a scholar of ancient paganism:

> Unfortunately, for many rituals we have only flawed documentation, from Christian clerics who found the rites appalling or racist anthropologists who sneered at them as the work of foolish primitives. Often the true intentions behind ceremonies dismissed as blasphemy or "fertility rites"—as if continuing life weren't important—have not come down to us. Even the most sympathetic observers can only guess at the awe and religious ecstasy produced by any ritual.[36]

Primary source material is simply not explicit enough to warrant the confident assertions of *The Da Vinci Code*. As on many topics, Dan Brown overstates his case. He lacks the necessary information to be so certain.

The novel and its author also fail to address the dark aspects of Hieros Gamos. This failure comes across in two ways. On the one hand, *The Da Vinci Code* leaves out horrifying details from both ancient and modern practice of the ritual. Here are two examples, the first from Ronald Nash and the second from Ms. Harline:

Cybele, also known as the Great Mother, was worshiped through much of the Hellenistic world. She undoubtedly began as a goddess of nature. Her early worship included orgiastic ceremonies in which her frenzied male worshipers were led to castrate themselves, following which they became "Galli" or eunuch-priests of the goddess. Cybele eventually came to be viewed as the Mother of all gods and the mistress of all life.[37]

The puberty rites of boys of the Marind-anim of New Guinea ended with a beautifully dressed, oiled and painted virgin being made to lie beneath a log platform, whereupon all the new initiates had sex with her before the assembled crowd. While the boy chosen as last lay with her, the ritualists jerked out the platform's supports. The logs fell on the pair, crushing them. The people retrieved the bodies, butchered and roasted them, and the crowd ate the young couple's flesh.

The Da Vinci Code also adopts a very naive attitude about sexual rituals, even if one ignores the gruesome realities about castration and killing. Consider the image of Hieros Gamos presented in the novel: beautifully dressed men and women engaged in religion-inspired sex. Robert Langdon argued that Hieros Gamos only "*looked* like a sex ritual" and "had nothing to do with eroticism."

In his haste to comfort Sophie, distressed over the memory of her grandfather's participation in the rite, Langdon forgets the fundamental premise of Heiros Gamos: to celebrate the sexual union of males and females and honour the erotic impulse behind all of creation. Beyond this contradiction, Dan Brown is simply oblivious to the obvious.

Humans who engage in any form of Hieros Gamos are involved in a sex ritual, and it will have a lot to do with eroticism. Further, there will be a price to pay, emotionally, physically, and spiritually. This can be seen clearly through any study of contemporary religious movements that have encouraged group sex or have mandated that males and/or females participate in sexual union with the relevant guru, priestess, or pastor.

Readers who want to investigate this matter further can study firsthand reports of those who have taken part in the sex rites of Hindu leader Sai Baba and the controversial guru Adi Da, who lives on a remote Fiji island. In *Traveller in Space* June Campbell tells of her life as a sexual consort to a major Tibetan Buddhist master. Even more horrific are the accounts of sacred prostitution and religion-based incest in the early days of The Children of God (now called the Family International), founded by David Berg (a.k.a. Moses David and Father) in the late sixties.[38]

Conclusion

The Da Vinci Code cannot be taken seriously as a guide to the study of sexual ritual related to religion. The novel has a simplistic picture of ancient and modern paganism. It totally misrepresents sexual practices in ancient Judaism and early Christianity. It is even wrong in its underlying suggestions that Gnostic Christians were sexual libertarians.

On a deeper level, Dan Brown is surely bluffing in his rhetoric about Hieros Gamos. It is hard to imagine that he really believes his own novel's ideology. Would he be willing to participate in the ancient ritual that *The Da Vinci Code* defends? Would he really recommend the ancient ritual to his wife, family, and friends?

Chapter Eight

Witches, the Illuminati, Masons and Opus Dei

O ccult themes surface frequently in Dan Brown's writings. *The Da Vinci Code* is preoccupied with general pagan themes but also makes some very strident claims about witches, masons, and members of Opus Dei. Brown's earlier novel *Angels & Demons* deals explicitly with the Masons and the Illuminati. How accurate are Brown's views? We will examine his views about witchcraft and then deal with the "secret" societies.

Witches and the Vatican

The Da Vinci Code actually defends a general theory about witchcraft that both witches and Christians do not believe. By this I refer to the view, noted in the last chapter, that Jesus and the earliest Christians were actually pagans or witches. Brown would find it impossible to find a serious scholar who argues for this understanding of history. The novel is also careless on specifics about witchcraft.

According to the novel, witches were not guarded by the powerful Priory of Sion and therefore experienced the full wrath of the Vatican. This was "a brutal crusade to 'reeducate' the pagan and feminine-worshipping religions." *The Da Vinci Code* then states:

The Catholic Inquisition published the book that arguably could be called the most blood-soaked publication in human history. *Malleus Maleficarum*—or *The Witches' Hammer*—indoctrinated the world to "the dangers of freethinking women" and instructed the clergy how to locate, torture, and destroy them.

Those deemed "witches" by the Church included all female scholars, priestesses, gypsies, mystics, nature lovers, herb gatherers, and any women "suspiciously attuned to the natural world." Midwives also were killed for their heretical practice of using medical knowledge to ease the pain of childbirth—a suffering, the Church claimed, that was God's rightful punishment for Eve's partaking of the Apple of Knowledge, thus giving birth to the idea of Original Sin.

During three hundred years of witch hunts, the Church burned at the stake an astounding five *million* women.

There are two major blunders in the novel's polemic about the Vatican attack on witchcraft. First, there is a huge mistake about the scope of the Inquisition. Dan Brown puts the number of deaths at five million. Historians who specialize in the study of witchcraft now consistently state that the number is actually no more than 100,000—a staggering figure, and horrible, but nowhere near five million.[39]

The novel also significantly distorts the nature of the Church polemic against the alleged witches. The attack was not about "the dangers of freethinking women" or about female scholars, gypsies, priestesses, mystics, nature lovers, herb gatherers, midwives, or "women 'suspiciously attuned to the natural world.'"

The Da Vinci Code spins a verbal web to make it look like persecution of witches was essentially an attack on female pagan scholars and female nature lovers. Dan Brown neglects to mention that males were also targeted as witches. Further, nowhere in the novel do we hear the fact that accusations against alleged female witches were often made by females.

The novel also misleads readers by creating the impression that the assault on witches was basically an operation of the

Vatican. Protestants were just as involved in the persecution of alleged witches, and in some areas of Europe Protestant leaders killed more accused witches than did Catholic inquisitors.

Of course, there is no denying the involvement of the Vatican. Some Catholic critics of *The Da Vinci Code* have tried to whitewash the issue by arguing that witches were put to death by the state and not the Church. This is simply disingenuous. While secular courts were often harder on witches than the Inquisition courts, no amount of denial can obscure the obvious fact that the Catholic Church engaged in the persecution, torture, and killing of witches.

The most significant fact to remember about the witchcraft hysteria is that Church officials and lay Christians believed that witchcraft was real and that it was essentially about Satanism, radical evil power, and unimaginable wicked deeds. The *Malleus Maleficarum* and other similar treatises speak against witches who slaughter babies, have sex with demons, poison their neighbours, and bring plagues to countries.

What about the underlying premise of *The Da Vinci Code* that those accused of witchcraft were actually practitioners of ancient paganism who were simply celebrating sexuality and the sacred feminine? This was once a popular theory, one that argued for a continuing line of witches from ancient to modern times. Thus, ancient pagan followers of Isis were like witches in the Middle Ages, who were similar to modern-day wiccans. Modern witches are beginning to realize the flimsy evidence for this viewpoint.[40]

In other words, one must make clear distinctions between the actual beliefs and practices of ancient pagans, the so-called witches of Europe and colonial America, and today's witchcraft community. Crucial distinctions must also be noted about contemporary witchcraft. In terms of broad categories, there are four types of witchcraft in our world:

- *Witchcraft* can refer to the practice of sorcery done by witch doctors in pre-industrial, non-technological societies.
- *Witchcraft* is also the term given to those who follow the pagan path idolized in *The Da Vinci Code*. Such witches

worship gods and goddesses, honour Mother Earth, participate in covens, celebrate sexuality in their rituals, and follow the cycles of nature for their holy days.

- There also witches who call themselves Satanists. They follow "the dark side" and believe that true living involves being self-centred and engaging in all the lusts of the flesh. This type of witchcraft is exemplified by Anton LaVey, the founder of the Church of Satan and author of *The Satanic Bible*. LaVey claimed that he did not actually believe in Satan but used the term to celebrate his anti-Christian lifestyle.

- Finally, there are witches who actually worship Satan, call themselves Satanists, and engage in Satanic Ritual Abuse. They form a criminal element in various countries of the world. Usually such Satanists operate as loners or in wicked concert with a handful of others. Some serial killers represent themselves as Satanists.

Dan Brown does not make the mistake of confusing ordinary witches and Satanists. He does fail, however, by drawing a direct equation between ancient pagans, Mary Magdalene, witches of the Middle Ages, and modern followers of "white" witchcraft. Further, there is no evidence that modern pagans engage in practices that predate the late 19th century. Most rituals that take place in contemporary covens were created by Gerald Gardner (1884–1964), the founder of modern witchcraft in the West.[41]

The Illuminati

Though Dan Brown states that he is not a fan of conspiracy theories, his rhetoric about the Illuminati in *Angels & Demons* makes his claim hard to believe. According to Brown the Illuminati has become one of the most powerful secret societies on earth. Here are some of his most significant claims:

1. *The Illuminati started in the 1500s in Rome*
2. *It was originally a group of scientists who wanted to resist the anti-scientific bias of the Church*

3. *They were hunted ruthlessly by the Vatican*

4. *The Illuminati met in a secret lair they called the Church of Illumination*

5. *Galileo was their most famous member*

6. *The Illuminati turned criminal after four early members were arrested and tortured*

7. *The Vatican referred to the secret society as* Shaitan, *the Islamic term for adversary (which is the root for the English word* Satan*)*

8. *John Milton was a member of the Illuminati*

9. *Bavarian Freemasons sheltered the Illuminati*

10. *Masons became an unwitting front for the Illuminati*

11. *The Illuminati infiltrated early American Masonry*

12. *The Illuminati goal is a secular New World Order*

13. *United States currency is covered with Illuminati symbols (courtesy of Vice President Henry Wallace, a leading Mason)*

14. *The Illuminati has infiltrated the Vatican and the English Parliament*

15. *The Illuminati was involved in Marxism and the Russian Revolution*

16. *Winston Churchill warned about the Illuminati*

17. *U.S. President Woodrow Wilson was alarmed about the Illuminati*

18. *Cecil Rhodes was an Illuminati, and the Rhodes scholarship was set up to recruit members*

19. *The death of John Paul I was probably the work of the Illuminati*

20. *George Bush, a prominent Mason, shut down the CIA investigation of the Illuminati*

Before commenting on the specifics, some preliminary observations are important. First, the reader will notice that all of these items are about actual people and/or events. Brown states at the outset of *Angels & Demons* that "the brotherhood of the Illuminati is factual."

Second, Brown clearly does not hesitate to make the most astounding assertions, with no hint of modesty or uncertainty. Readers should think carefully about how it is possible that a man who has spent most of his life as an English teacher and a novelist could know so much about some of the most complicated and controversial issues addressed by humans.

Third, there is also something intrinsically alarming about the nature and trajectory of Dan Brown's speculations about the Illuminati and Freemasonry. He provides virtually no evidence or resource material so that readers can check the authenticity of his claims. Further, there is the danger that readers will follow his path and launch into the endless and unproductive world of Illuminati speculation.

What about the specifics in Dan Brown's portrait of the Illuminati? A blunt verdict is necessary. Most of his claims are virtually worthless. He is not even correct on the origin of the secret society. The Illuminati did not start in the time of Galileo. Rather, in 1776 Dr. Adam Weishaupt, a canon law professor at Ingolstadt University in Bavaria, founded a secret society known as the Order of the Illuminati. There may have been connections with Bavarian Masonry. Weishaupt's Illuminati group was suppressed by the government in 1785.

There is no evidence of an earlier Illuminati connected with Galileo and John Milton.[42] Brown's whole discussion about Vatican suppression of the Illuminati is baseless. Further, *Shaitan* is not the root word for Satan. It is the term for Satan in various versions of the Qur'an. Both *Shaitan* and Satan are from a Hebrew word that means adversary.

Brown's postulations about alleged Illuminati involvement in the Vatican, the English Parliament, the Russian Revolution, the makeup of American currency, etc., must be treated as total speculation. As with other Illuminati theorists, he can provide no primary evidence for the existence of the Illuminati after 1785. Further, Brown is hard pressed to prove that his version of the Illuminati is closer to reality than the alternative views of fellow conspirators.

Brown's suggestion about Illuminati influence on American currency is entirely without merit since he cannot prove the existence of a modern-day Illuminati. The popular idea that Henry Wallace influenced President Roosevelt to choose Masonic symbols for the one dollar bill is simply a case for Masonic involvement, not Illuminati influence. Further, the history of symbols on American currency is complicated and cannot be explained simply by involvement of early Masons (Benjamin Franklin) or later ones (Henry Wallace).

Dan Brown and the Masons

Alarm about Masonic symbols is only possible in Brown's novel because of the social context of underlying and widespread suspicion about Freemasonry. Conspiracy theories about Masons started to circulate soon after the formation of the first Grand Lodge in London on June 24, 1717. Roman Catholic popes have condemned Masonry, and many Protestant denominations forbid membership in the Lodge.[43]

Accusations against the Lodge are largely a result of fabrication and poor research on the part of careless and extreme critics. For example, the charge that Albert Pike, a leading nineteenth century Masonic scholar, advocated the worship of Lucifer is an outright lie. The hoax against Pike was started by Leo Taxil, a pen name for Gabriel Antoine Jogand-Pages, an anti-Masonic writer who invented a quote from Pike to carry on a vendetta against the Lodge.

While Masons are to care for fellow members, their oaths forbid them to break the law or harbour any criminal. Accusations about Masonic murders are strong in only one case, a famous one involving ex-Mason William Morgan. This New York resident was killed in 1826, probably at the hands of a few zealous Masons upset at Morgan for revealing their secret rituals.

Readers of *The Da Vinci Code* and *Angels & Demons* can be cured of conspiracy theories about Freemasonry and the Illuminati by surfing the Internet and exposing themselves to the endless and contradictory claims about both groups. This can be a very depressing exercise, especially when allegations about the Illuminati and Masons are used to target Jews, Muslims, and blacks.

Opus Dei

Interest in the Catholic movement known as Opus Dei has increased dramatically because of its central place in the plot line of *The Da Vinci Code*. Though Dan Brown claims to have done a lot of research on the movement, scholars who have studied the movement do not share the very nasty picture of Opus Dei presented in the novel.

Yes, there are people who have not enjoyed their time in Opus Dei. Further, the group seems to many to be too strict in its regimen for members. These appropriate items are explored on the Opus Dei Awareness Network.[44] However, these points are insignificant when contrasted with the dark picture presented in the novel. There the plot is about conspiracy theories, assault, assassination, murder, lies, political manipulations, and Vatican intrigue.

While the final part of the novel offers a softer view of Opus Dei, it is regrettable that Dan Brown included a reference on page one to the movement. Why is it necessary to mention the U.S.A. address of Opus Dei as a relevant fact in a novel? It looks like this was done to give the impression that the novel is based on fact. It is, as we have seen repeatedly, a work of fiction that makes abundant factual errors about the religious and historical issues it raises.[45]

Conclusion

Dan Brown's *Angels & Demons* and *The Da Vinci Code* make great reading as thriller novels. However, both volumes fail at the intellectual and historical level because of their advance of erroneous theories about witchcraft, the Illuminati, Masons, and Opus Dei. Brown's wild speculations and careless research are no cause for celebration, no matter how long his novels remain on the bestseller lists.

Conclusion

An Open Letter to Dan Brown

Dear Dan,   March 7, 2005

We have never met though, as mentioned in my book, we both know Martyn Percy, the Anglican scholar. I was going to write a conclusion that stated that no number of replies to *The Da Vinci Code* will do much to stop millions from believing its radical and misleading theories about Jesus, Mary Magdalene, the Gnostic Gospels, Constantine and the Bible, the Priory of Sion, and so on. I then realized that statement was not true. In fact, you could correct the serious mistakes you have made in your book. These errors have hurt people both spiritually and intellectually.

So, that is why I am sending this open letter to you. I defend your freedom to believe and write what you want. I admire your discipline as a writer. I also noted earlier in this book that you seem like a really nice guy, based on what I have seen of you in documentaries and in television interviews. I know that you had no idea that *The Da Vinci Code* would become one of the best-selling books of all time. I am sure that you never imagined that you would become one of the most influential spiritual writers of our new century.

With this powerful platform and influence comes a solemn responsibility. Dan, I urge you to reconsider many of the views that you have advanced in both *The Da Vinci Code* and *Angels & Demons*. You claim to be a follower of Jesus Christ. You also claim that you believe in doing careful and exhaustive research. Given both of these claims, I believe you owe it to your readers and to Christ to reconsider your theories.

I am not questioning your motives or judging your heart. Rather, I am trying to get you to see that many of the ideas in your two novels are inconsistent with what it means to be a Christian and what it means to do careful research and thinking. So far, you have simply avoided answering your critics. You seem largely content to rest on your popularity. In your occasional public comments you rely on very superficial arguments to defend views and ideas that are false, irrational, unhistorical, and anti-Christian.

At one point you mention that "history has been written by the winners." You use this line to promote your radical theories about early Christianity, about Jesus and Mary Magdalene, about Constantine, and about the Priory of Sion. Dan, no Gnostic writers (the so-called losers in history) believed your views about Jesus or about sex rituals. There are no early documents about Christians protecting the bones of Mary. No scholars of Roman history share your views on Constantine. Dan, the real Priory of Sion is an invention of that notorious fraud Pierre Plantard in this very century. Art historians uniformly dismiss your unique theories about Leonardo da Vinci. Have you asked yourself why that is so?

I am concerned that you have never admitted you have made a single mistake. Let me raise just two specific examples. Your novel states that there are 666 panes of glass in the pyramid entrance to the Louvre and that former French President Francois Mitterrand requested this number. Dan, a spokesperson for the architect who designed the entrance states that both claims are totally false. Will you now admit this error?

James Robinson, one of the great scholars of Gnosticism, has said that your views on Gnostic literature are unreliable. Are you open to his correction?

More seriously, do you truly believe that Jesus did not claim to be the Son of God? Why does the entire New Testament teach this? It is historically verifiable that the classical Christian Gospels were written long before the Gnostic literature. Why would you trust later material done by Gnostics who did not even know Jesus? Dan, if Jesus and Mary were actually married and had a child named Sarah, why is it that no one has mentioned this until our day? You have used neither primary historical material nor new evidence to support your claims. You need to admit your radical views about Jesus and Mary and their alleged French lineage are completely unhistorical, whether history is written by winners or losers.

You have also defended a totally bogus view of sex rituals as it relates to Judaism, Jesus, and the early Church. Dan, the Old Testament clearly does not advocate sex in the temple. It emphatically condemns it! Likewise, early Christians were never encouraged to have sacred orgies in church. You have been completely fooled by crackpots on this topic. You are absolutely correct that sex is a beautiful creation of God. Given this, you need to rethink the novel's defense of sex ritual in worship. If not, are you going to be consistent and join some radical witchcraft group that engages in the practice?

Dan, Christians from all over the world are finding that your novel is being used to attack the basic claims of the gospel. I am not talking here about your proper appreciation of sex and the beauty of the feminine. Rather, people now use *The Da Vinci Code* to prove that the Bible is not accurate and that Jesus is not the Son of God, performed no miracles, and was really a pagan. Are these your views? If not, you need to speak out clearly as a Christian about your unity with the clear teachings of the gospel and with fellow Christians.

I am sure it is distressful to have books like mine challenging and attacking your views. However, these responses to you rise directly from your statement on page one of *The Da Vinci Code* claiming your references to art, architecture, and ritual are accurate. I believe that the case against the accuracy of your intellectual and spiritual arguments is overwhelming. Dan, you have been fooled by conspiracy buffs like Plantard and have been misled by faulty research, especially from the authors of *Holy Blood, Holy Grail*.

For the sake of truth, I urge you to reconsider your errant views and warn your readers all over the world that your novel should simply be treated as nothing more than a novel. Your fame now gives you an incredible platform, an opportunity, and a duty to revise your views and respond carefully to the implications of your Christian commitment.

With best wishes,

James A. Beverley

Associate Director
Institute for the Study of American Religion
Santa Barbara, California

Professor
Tyndale Seminary
Toronto, Canada

jamesbeverley@sympatico.ca

The Deceptions of *The Da Vinci Code*

Contrary to the novel:

1. *Christianity is not built on fabrication.*
2. *The earliest Christians believed Jesus was the son of God.*
3. *Jesus was not a pagan or a witch.*
4. *The miracles of Jesus should be interpreted literally and at face value.*
5. *There is no historical evidence that Jesus married Mary Magdalene.*
6. *They did not have a child name Sarah.*
7. *No dynasty from Jesus or Mary Magdalene merged with French Kings.*
8. *Christians did not create Jesus from pagan religions.*
9. *There was no smear campaign against Mary Magdalene in the early church.*
10. *There is no proof that material about Mary was edited out of the Bible.*
11. *There are not countless references about Jesus being married to Mary.*
12. *There is no primary historical evidence that St. Peter was jealous of Mary.*
13. *There is no proof that Mary came from royalty.*

14. *The text of the Bible has been preserved carefully through the centuries.*

15. *The Bible was not invented by Constantine.*

16. *Constantine was not forced to be baptized.*

17. *The Council of Nicea did not invent the deity of Jesus.*

18. *Constantine did not invent the term heretic.*

19. *Constantine did not burn other Bibles.*

20. *The Gnostic Gospels are not more reliable than the four Christian Gospels.*

21. *The Dead Sea Scrolls do not provide information about Jesus Christ.*

22. *The Gnostic Gospels are written much later than the Christian Gospels.*

23. *The Gnostic Christians do not have the same view of Jesus as* The Da Vinci Code.

24. *The Gnostic Gospels do not offer a rich view of Jesus.*

25. *The Gnostic Gospels have no deep interest in the historical Jesus.*

26. *The Dead Sea Scrolls do not contradict classical Christian teaching.*

27. *There is no Priory of Sion that dates back to 1099.*

28. *Pierre Plantard started the Priory of Sion in 1956.*

29. *The Bibliothèque Nationale did not discover ancient documents about the Priory.*

30. *Pierre Plantard invented conspiracy theories about the Priory of Sion.*

31. *Plantard's false views were spread by the book* Holy Blood, Holy Grail.

32. The Da Vinci Code *is built on Plantard's lies.*

33. *The Holy Grail has always been viewed as the cup at the Last Supper.*

34. *The Knights Templar protected Jerusalem, not the bones of Mary Magdalene.*

35. *Leonardo was not a member of the Priory of Sion.*

36. *There is absolutely no proof that Leonardo was a member of any sex cult.*

37. *Leonardo was not that interested in religion.*

38. *Art scholars dismiss Dan Brown's eccentric interpretations of Leonardo.*

39. *It is John the Beloved beside Jesus in* **The Last Supper** *(not Mary Magdalene)*

40. *Jews did not condone sex orgies in the Temple.*

41. *Early Christians did not condone sexual ritual in worship.*

42. *Jews and early Christians were not pagans or witches.*

43. *Ancient sex rituals were very destructive to women.*

44. *Sex rituals in worship are very harmful to healthy sexuality.*

45. *The Catholic Inquisition did not kill 5 million witches.*

46. *Those targeted as witches were not freethinking nature lovers.*

47. *The Illuminati did not start in the time of Galileo.*

48. *There is no proof that the Illuminati still exists.*

49. *There are not 666 separate panes of glass in the entrance to the Louvre.*

50. *President Mitterrand did not order 666 panes of glass for the entrance.*

Endnotes

Chapter One: Inventing a New Jesus

[1]On the significance of Jesus, see Jaroslav Pelikan, *Jesus Through the Centuries* (New Haven: Yale, 1985).

[2] See the news report on this by Mark Hayward in *The Union Leader & New Hampshire Sunday News* (May 19, 2004).

[3] For a discussion of the inconsistency of calling oneself a Christian and not believing basic Christianity, see the discussions in Martin Gardner, *The Whys of a Philosophical Scrivener* (New York: Quill, 1983).

[4] *The New York Times* reported on February 19, 2005, that Brown's views on Leonardo were being dismissed by scholars at a meeting in Vinci, the hometown of the famous artist.

[5] See the discussion in Craig Blomberg, *Jesus and the Gospels* (Nashville: Broadman & Holman, 1997), p. 396.

[6] For extended critiques of various copycat theories, see Glenn Miller's work at www.christian-thinktank.com.

[7] Lewis had a positive impact on the fantasy writing of his friend J.R.R. Tolkien. Note A.N. Wilson's *C.S. Lewis: A Biography* (London: Collins, 1990), pp. 116–117.

[8] On complexities about Mithras, see the work of David Ulansey, *The Origins of the Mithraic Mysteries* (New York: Oxford, 1991).

[9] On the historical reliability of the Gospels, see James Dunn, *The Evidence for Jesus* (London: SCM, 1985) and Lee Strobel, *The Case for Christ* (Grand Rapids: Zondervan, 1998). In relation to Dan Brown's novel, see the arguments in Hank Hanegraaff and Paul Maier, *The Da Vinci Code: Truth or Fiction?* (Wheaton: Tyndale, 2004).

Chapter Two: Mary Magdalene: A New Goddess?

[10] For careful discussion on Mary Magdalene, note Darrell L. Bock, *Breaking The Da Vinci Code* (Nashville: Thomas Nelson, 2004), pp. 13–30.

[11] The idea that Mary Magdalene was a prostitute gained popularity only after its promotion by Pope Gregory I in 591 A.D. For a refutation of Dan Brown's confused understanding on Mary Magdalene, see Amy Welborn, *Decoding Da Vinci* (Huntington: Our Sunday Visitor, 2004), pp. 66–68.

[12] On the anti-Catholic bias, see Carl E. Olson & Sandra Miesel, *The Da Vinci Hoax* (San Francisco: Ignatius, 2004), pp. 294–295.

[13] For important Web sites, see www.magdalene.org, www.northernway.org, www.futurechurch.org, and www.gnosis.org.

Chapter Three: The Bible and the Ghost of Constantine

[14] For careful discussion on how we got the Bible, see Ben Witherington III, *The Gospel Code* (Downers Grove: InterVarsity, 2004), pp. 113–130.

[15] The scholars who study Constantine consistently point out how hard it was for him to make sudden and radical changes in the Roman Empire. The idea that he could get the whole Christian world to quickly change their views on the identity of Jesus is absurd. For discussion of Constantine's need for caution, see the entry on him in the current edition of the Encylopedia Britannica, by J.F. Matthews (Oxford University) and Donald MacGillivray Nicol (University of London).

[16] For expert writing on Constantine and paganism, see the works of Ramsey MacMullen, professor emeritus at Yale University. See, for example, his work *Constantine* (1987) and *Christianizing the Roman Empire* (1986).

[17] For quotations from the early Church leaders, see the searchable database at www.ccel.org/fathers2 and note the work by J.N.D. Kelly, *Early Christian Doctrines* (New York: Harper & Row, 1978). Kelly's book simply blows apart the views of Dan Brown on the way that the early Church viewed Jesus.

[18] *The Cambridge History of the Bible* is presented in three volumes. For other careful work on the subject, see G.C. Berkouwer, *Holy Scripture* (Grand Rapids: Eerdmans, 1975), pp. 66–104.

Chapter Four: Hidden Gospels?

[19] See James Robinson, ed., *The Nag Hammadi Library*, rev. ed. (San Francisco: Harper, 1990.

[20] For a scholarly critique of Pagels, note the discussions about her in Ben Witherington III, *The Gospel Code*, passim.

[21] Thankfully, most of the Gnostic material is searchable on-line at various sites, including at the Gnostic Society Library Web site (www.gnosis.org).

[22] See the interview with Pagels in Dan Burstein, *Secrets of the Code* (New York: CDS, 2004), pp. 100–105. Pagels is very negative on traditional Christians who are careless with facts, while she has little criticism of Brown for his utterly ridiculous views that have no support in either the traditional Gospels or in the Gnostic texts.

[23] See Birger A. Pearson, "The Other Christians," *The New York Review of Books* (October 23, 2003).

[24] Robinson, in *Secrets of the Code*, p. 98.

[25] For scholarly discussion about the Dead Sea Scrolls, see the recommendations at the Gnostic Society Library Web site (http://www.gnosis.org). Also, consult the research on the Scrolls from Craig Evans, Professor of New Testament at Acadia Divinity College, Nova Scotia.

Chapter Five: Secret Societies and the Holy Grail

[26] It is quite significant that the publisher of the Italian version of *The Da Vinci Code* removed this page claiming factuality from later editions.

[27] For a careful and powerful critique of the myths about the Priory of Sion and related issues, see the Web site material from Massimo Introvigne, one of the great scholars of contemporary religious movements. See www.cesnur.org for Massimo's research.

[28] On Isaac Newton, see the essay by Freeman Dyson in *The New York Review of Books* (July 3, 2003).

[29] See http://priory-of-sion.com for the amazing research provided by Paul Smith.

[30] Dan Brown shows no concerns at all that he contradicts all previous understandings of what was meant by the Holy Grail. For scholarly study, see Richard Barber, *The Holy Grail* (Cambridge: Harvard, 2004).

Chapter Six: The Real Leonardo da Vinci

[31] For a typical art historian's verdict on Dan Brown, see the review by Bruce Boucher, Art Institute of Chicago, in *The New York Times* (8/3/2003).

[32] Da Vinci is mentioned only twice in Kenneth Latourette's 1500-page book *A History of Christianity* (New York: Harper & Row, 1955).

[33] Consult the evidence provided in Richard Abanes, *The Truth Behind the Da Vinci Code* (Eugene: Harvest House, 2004), pp. 70–71.

Chapter Seven: Sex at the Altar

[34] For a non-sexual interpretation of Gothic architecture, see Robert A. Scott, *The Gothic Enterprise* (University of Southern California Press, 2003).

[35] For scholarly and careful understanding of orthodox Jewish views of God and sexuality, see Hayim Halevy Donin, *To Be a Jew* (New York: Basic, 2001). I am grateful to my colleague John Kessler, Professor of Old Testament, Tyndale Seminary, for his help on Hebrew language issues raised by Brown. John has a doctorate from the Sorbonne.

[36] See Miriam Harline's research at www.widdershins.org/vol5iss3/01.htm.

[37] Ronald Nash provides careful assessment of the relationship between Christianity and pagan views and rites in an essay for *Christian Research Journal* (Winter 1994).

[38] For data on these groups and individuals, see the relevant sections of my *Nelson's Illustrated Guide to Religions* (Nashville: Thomas Nelson, 2005).

Chapter Eight: Witches, the Illuminati, Masons and Opus Dei

[39] For scholarly data, see Brian P. Levack, *The Witch-Hunt in Early Modern Europe* (New York: Addison-Wesley, 1995) and Jeffrey B. Russell, *A History of Witchcraft* (New York: Thames and Hudson, 1980).

[40] On this, see Charlotte Allen, "The Scholars and the Goddess," *The Atlantic Monthly* (January 2001).

[41] The most scholarly work on the history of modern witchcraft is Ronald Hutton, *The Triumph of the Moon* (London: Oxford University Press, 1999).

[42] The great scholars of Galileo and Milton never mention any possible involvement in a secret Illuminati. For an overview on Galileo, see William Shea's essay in David Lindberg and Ronald Numbers, eds., *God and Nature* (Berkeley: University of California Press, 1986), pp. 114–135. Readers can also consult The Galileo Project at Rice University. The term *Illuminati* is not even mentioned in the list of subjects for the *The Milton Encyclopedia*, edited by Professor Thomas N. Corns, forthcoming from Yale University Press.

[43] I urge readers to be very careful in trusting popular books against the Masons. A careful critique of some elements of their rituals is provided by Steve Tsoukalas in *Masonic Rites and Wrongs* (Phillipsburg: Presbyterian & Reformed Publishing Co., 1995).

[44] See www.odan.org.

[45] Opus Dei has a reply to *The Da Vinci Code* at www.opusdei.org.

A Guide to Books on *The DaVinci Code*

I am an evangelical Christian scholar and am glad to recommend the works of fellow evangelicals. I have learned a lot from their research. These books are *Breaking The Da Vinci Code* (Darrell Bock), *Cracking Da Vinci's Code* (James Garlow & Peter Jones), *The Da Vinci Code: Fact or Fiction?* (Hank Hanegraaff & Paul Maier), *The Da Vinci Deception* (Erwin Lutzer), *The Gospel Code* (Ben Witherington III), and *The Truth Behind the Da Vinci Code* (Richard Abanes).

There are at least three Catholic responses. *The Da Vinci Code Hoax* (Carl Olson and Sandra Meisel) is the most exhaustive. Amy Welborn's *De-Coding Da Vinci* has a lot of useful data. Steven Kellmeyer reacts to various claims in the order that they are presented in Dan Brown's novel. See his *Fact and Fiction in the Da Vinci Code*.

Bart D. Ehrman's *Truth and Fiction in The Da Vinci Code* is written from the point of view of a historian of early Christianity. It is well done and offers careful critique of Dan Brown's theories.

Several books have been written in support of Dan Brown's theories. Both Simon Cox (*Cracking the Da Vinci Code*) and Martin Lunn (*Da Vinci Code Decoded*) take this approach. I find myself totally unconvinced by their attempts to endorse and even go beyond what is claimed in *The Da Vinci Code*.

Two books attempt to provide background information on all the data and issues in the novel. Betsy Eble does this in *Depth and Details*. More significant, Dan Burstein covers a lot of issues in his *Secrets of the Code*. Burstein provides articles and essays from various writers and does interviews as well. However, the book is radically marred in the fact that it does not provide a guide on which writers to trust on all the various topics.

A Note on the Author

James A. Beverley is Associate Director of the Institute for the Study of American Religion in Santa Barbara, California, and professor at Tyndale Seminary in Toronto, Canada. He is the senior editor of the forthcoming *HarperCollins' Encyclopedia of Religions in Canada* and the author of the forthcoming 700-page *Nelson's Illustrated Guide to Religions*. He has also written three books on Islam and two books on charismatic Christianity.

He is a specialist on the study of new religions and did his Ph.D. thesis on the inner teachings of Sun Myung Moon. He has been interviewed frequently by the media, including BBC radio, Finnish television, CBC Radio, *The Los Angeles Times*, CBC television, Syrian television, CTV News, *The Globe & Mail*, etc. He has written for *Christianity Today* magazine, including a cover story on Islam and an article based on his personal interview with His Holiness the Dalai Lama in India. Professor Beverley has taught at colleges and universities in Canada, the U.S., Africa, and India.

Professor Beverley is a member of the American Academy of Religion, the Evangelical Theological Society, the Canadian Society for the Study of Religion, the Evangelical Philosophical Society, and the Society for the Scientific Study of Religion. His expert opinion has been sought in both criminal and civil trials, including the case of Holocaust denier Malcolm Ross. His testimony in a Toronto criminal case was included in a television documentary.

Professor Beverley holds an Honors B.A. in Philosophy (Acadia University, 1974), Master of Divinity (Acadia, 1977), Master of Theology (University of Toronto, 1983) and Ph.D. (University of Saint Michael's College, 1994). During his doctoral work Professor Beverley studied with Hans Küng, the famous Catholic scholar, and Antony Flew, one of the world's leading philosophers.

His wife Gloria is a kindergarten teacher in the Ontario public school system. Jim and Gloria have two adult children. Andrea is doing a Ph.D. in English literature, and Derek is completing a Bachelor's degree in Fine Arts at the Ontario College of Art and Design.